NOTHING

—— **HAS A** ——

FACE

LEADING

AT EVERY LEVEL

FIRST EDITION

Earl L. Gay, RADM (ret) | JoeDae Jenkins | Dr. Gerald Gray | Mark A. Hopkins | Earl S. Gray, Jr. | Dr. Marsha Donaldson

WE DELIVER - 633 - YOU DECIDE

INTRODUCTION

The Power of People

In every organization, institution, family, church, community, and walk of life, we naturally identify a leader. Sometimes that leader is chosen formally through titles, elections, or appointments. Other times, leadership emerges informally when someone steps up to guide, support, and inspire.

We often think of leadership as something that exists at the top: the corner office, the pulpit, the head of the table. But here is a truth worth remembering: there is no "top" without the people who stand beneath it, beside it, and around it. Leadership does not exist in isolation; it exists in relationship.

Authentic leadership moves in every direction, upward and downward, outward and inward. It is not only about guiding those who follow but also about influencing and inspiring those who lead beside or above us. Every position in the chain matters, and the chain is only as strong as its connections.

When we commit to leading at every level, we create a culture where everyone takes responsibility for the success of the whole. We build bridges instead of walls. We listen as much as we speak.

We lead not only through authority, but through service, example, and empathy.

This philosophy connects us. It reminds us that we are part of something bigger than ourselves. It shapes our perspective, humbles our decisions, and strengthens our resolve. In doing so, it molds us not only into better leaders but into better people.

The power of people is not found in a single role, but in the shared commitment to lift one another higher. That is how we create stronger organizations, healthier communities, and ultimately, a better world.

Leadership wears many faces, and each of us brings one shaped by a different journey. *Nothing Has a Face* was born from a shared conviction that leadership, at its core, is not a position or a process. It is profoundly human. In an age where technology, bureaucracy, and constant change threaten to strip leadership of its emotional connection, this book seeks to restore its humanity. It reminds us that transformation without people is motion without meaning.

Earl S. Gray Jr., a retired Navy Force Master Chief and corporate leader, brings more than three decades of experience guiding teams in high-stakes, high-pressure environments. His leadership was tested in the heat of combat and refined through years of commanding thousands across the military and private sectors.

Earl's chapters bring to life the principles of trust, accountability, and empowerment, lessons learned on the decks of ships, shore stations, and within the hearts of those he led.

Earl L. Gay, a retired two-star Admiral in the U.S. Navy and political appointee, contributes lessons forged through decades of service. From commanding warships and shore commands to mentoring future generations of leaders, his experience reveals that leadership is not about authority but about connection. Every decision, every success, and every command rests on trust and mutual respect. His voice offers a powerful perspective on leading with conviction, courage, and humility under pressure.

Dr. Marsha A. Donaldson, a psychologist, researcher, and organizational strategist, examines leadership through the lens of human behavior. She explores how empathy, data, and communication intersect to create sustainable change. Her insights challenge leaders to see transformation not as a technical exercise but as a human endeavor that requires listening, authenticity, and emotional intelligence.

JoeDae Jenkins, a Chancellor Judge and Pastor, contributes the voice of discernment and justice. He reveals how leadership must balance compassion with accountability. Through his perspective, we confront the unseen forces that drive resistance and learn that true authority is earned not by command but by character.

Dr. Gerald Gray, a clinical psychologist, leadership consultant, and retired Navy Captain Chaplain, explores the inner resilience of leaders. His chapters reveal that culture is not an abstract idea but a living force made up of people, beliefs, and shared values. He reminds us that leading others begins with mastering ourselves.

Mark A. Hopkins, a retired college professor, Navy Draftsman First Class Petty Officer, and lifelong mentor, closes the circle by focusing on communication, feedback, and legacy. His reflections teach that leadership endures when wisdom is shared and when data is paired with human stories. He shows that teaching and leading share the same purpose: to develop others.

Together, we wrote *Nothing Has a Face* as a call to rehumanize leadership at every level. The book is structured in four parts: understanding why change feels faceless, uncovering hidden forces, practicing human-centered transformation, and embedding that change into stories that last.

Each chapter invites you to pause, reflect, and write. The Reflection Prompts that follow each section are not academic exercises; they are pathways to self-awareness. They ask you to revisit moments of failure and triumph, to name the faces behind the work, and to rediscover the people who gave meaning to your leadership journey.

As you read, you will notice that our voices differ, one disciplined, one reflective, one judicial, one clinical, one instructional, yet they harmonize around a shared truth: leadership begins and ends with people.

We invite you to look beyond the systems, structures, and titles. See the human faces. See the stories. And perhaps, see your own reflected in every chapter that follows.

PREFACE

Leadership is both simple and complex, fleeting in its presence yet lasting in its impact. Some of us have been fortunate to serve under great leaders, while others have only known poor ones. But every experience, whether guided by wisdom or marked by failure, teaches us something about who we are and who we can become. Leadership is a reflection of humanity in motion, shaped by values, culture, and the courage to serve.

As a two-star admiral in the United States Navy who retired in 2013, I learned that leadership is not confined to titles, ranks, or commands. It begins and ends with people: one team, one mission. I have held six commands, each different in scope, responsibility, and challenge, yet one truth remained constant. The strength of any organization lies in the unity of its team. When every individual, from the most senior officer to the janitor, feels like a stakeholder, the potential of that team becomes limitless.

Leadership demands mutual, unshakable trust. It must be built, not assumed. It must be earned, not demanded. And it must be maintained through integrity, consistency, and transparency. When trust is present, empowerment follows. When empowerment takes hold, initiative thrives. And when initiative thrives, leaders can step away, knowing the team will still function, perhaps even better, without them.

Throughout my journey, I have learned that no two leaders are alike. Our upbringings, experiences, and worldviews, whether forged in Alaska or Mississippi, shape how we lead and how we follow. Great leadership is not about perfection; it is about presence, humility, and the willingness to learn from every person and every moment. The best leaders are those who remain students of life: curious, compassionate, and adaptable.

As you read this book, I encourage you to take lessons from both the good and the bad leaders you encounter. Learn from their triumphs and their missteps. Notice what builds connection and what breaks it. Leadership, at its core, is about relationships, knowing your mission, articulating expectations, maintaining open communication, and believing deeply in the purpose that binds you to others.

When you find a good leader, or become one, hold fast to the traits that inspire and magnify them. Remember that leadership is never about the face of the leader, but about the faces of those who follow.

Earl L. Gay's Leadership Pearls of Wisdom

1. Everybody Becomes a Stakeholder

True leadership turns followers into stakeholders. When people believe they have a share in the mission, they invest their hearts, not just their hands. Ownership transforms compliance into commitment.

2. Mutual Trust Breeds Empowerment

Trust is the currency of leadership. When leaders trust their people and their people trust them in return, the results are exponential. Mutual trust gives birth to initiative, creativity, and courage.

3. There Are No Limits Once the Team Comes Together

When alignment and unity take root, momentum becomes unstoppable. Across six commands, I learned that once the team moves as one, even the impossible becomes routine.

4. Lessons Learned and Lessons Not Learned the Hard Way

Not every lesson needs to come with a scar. Wisdom is found in observation as much as in experience. Learn early, adapt quickly, and guide others to avoid the pitfalls you have already crossed.

5. Find the Commonality of the Team

Great teams are built on shared ground. Find what connects your people: purpose, respect, or vision, and use it as the foundation for everything you do together. Remember to recognize people, reward their hard work and remember the talent of the team.

6. Learn from Good Leaders and the Bad Ones Too

Every leader you encounter is a mirror. The good reflect what to emulate; the bad reveal what to avoid. Both sharpen your leadership edge if you are willing to study and listen.

7. Build a Team That Functions Without You

The ultimate measure of leadership is what happens when you are not there. A well-trained, trusted team should be able to execute at a high level. Leadership built on dependency is not leadership at all.

8. When the Chemistry Clicks on Day One

Sometimes the magic happens immediately. When your team naturally connects from the start, do not overthink it. Lean in, move with purpose, and use that early momentum to accelerate progress.

9. Ownership Breeds Leadership

People rise when they know they are accountable. Give them something meaningful to own and watch how their pride and performance multiply. Responsibility transforms effort into excellence.

10. Touchstones of Leadership: Engage with Everyone

Leadership is not a title; it is touch. The best leaders walk the floors, shake hands, listen to stories, and see people. Connection creates culture, and culture creates results.

11. Every Day Will Not Be Perfect

Challenges will come. That is the nature of leadership. You cannot prevent bad days, but you can prepare for them. Equip yourself and your team with these pearls of wisdom, and you will prevent most problems before they start. Preparation turns adversity into opportunity.

12. You Are Responsible

Leadership is accountability. When things go wrong, stand tall and take responsibility. When things go right, step back and give your team the credit. That balance earns respect and builds loyalty that lasts far beyond any single success.

CONTENTS

1

WHEN CHANGE HAS NO FACE

Change rarely knocks first. It arrives quietly: an email, a memo, a whispered conversation that spreads faster than facts. By the time the message reaches the people it affects most, the decision has already been made. No one knows exactly who made it. The language is polished with words like "strategic realignment," "restructuring," and "modernization," but the meaning feels hollow. Behind those words are hearts beating faster. Some feel fear. Others feel anger. Most feel unseen.

This is the anatomy of faceless change, transformation that moves through an organization, a community, or a life with no human face to guide it. It is not change itself that frightens people; it is invisible leadership. In every era, change has been both an incredible opportunity and a significant disruptor. What determines which it becomes is not the speed of innovation but the presence of humanity. When people cannot see the person behind the policy or the purpose behind the shift, change feels like a stranger, uninvited and unaccountable.

Faceless change makes people wonder:

> ⇒ Who decided this?

> ⇒ Does my voice matter?

> ⇒ What happens to me now?

These questions are not signs of resistance; they are signs of humanity. Yet too often, leaders mistake uncertainty for defiance and respond with more control, more jargon, and more distance, reinforcing the very fear they intended to calm.

Authentic leadership is not about removing emotion from the process; it is about walking through emotion with courage and clarity.

Every story of faceless change has an invisible architect, a committee, a board, or an executive team trying to do the right thing without being seen doing it. The intentions are rarely malicious. Often, they are rooted in efficiency, privacy, or the desire to avoid confrontation. But efficiency without empathy breeds alienation, and privacy without transparency breeds' mistrust.

Leadership consultant Simon Sinek once said, "People don't buy what you do; they buy why you do it." In the same way, people do not follow change because it is logical; they follow it because it is human.

When the "why" is missing, the "what" becomes unbearable. Faceless change is not just a communication problem; it is a crisis of connection. It erodes the social fabric that holds teams, families, and communities together. In psychology, diffusion of responsibility occurs when everyone assumes someone else will act, so no one acts. In organizations, faceless change is its twin. When no one person stands as the visible face of transformation, accountability evaporates. The result is emotional disorientation. People struggle to find reassurance or to know where to direct their questions.

Neuroscientists call this the "amygdala hijack," the survival system taking over when uncertainty feels like a threat.

What makes uncertainty stressful is not the lack of control but the lack of connection. Humans are wired for belonging. When leaders disappear behind processes, they unknowingly trigger the same neural pathways associated with abandonment. Faceless change makes people feel left behind, even when the intent was to move everyone forward.

A study in organizational psychology found that employees who feel excluded during change processes are five times more likely to disengage and seven times more likely to leave within a year. Yet when asked why, many do not cite the decision itself; they cite how it was delivered. People will forgive a tough decision if it is made with transparency and honesty. What they rarely forgive is silence.

Silence is not neutral. It communicates indifference. It suggests that those impacted are not worthy of context or compassion. Every system, whether corporate, educational, or governmental, faces the temptation of silence. It is faster. It is cleaner. But silence is the most expensive shortcut a leader can take. It costs trust. And trust, once lost, is the hardest currency to earn back.

Faceless change does not simply alter systems; it alters souls. It drains energy, creativity, and optimism from the people who are supposed to carry the change forward. When people are treated as objects of change instead of partners in it, they stop contributing. They comply, but they no longer care. They attend meetings, but their minds are elsewhere.

This quiet disengagement is often mistaken for stability. "At least no one's complaining," leaders tell themselves. But silence is not peace; it is retreat.

At the core of this withdrawal is a sense of invisibility. According to Maslow's hierarchy of needs, after safety and physiological security, the next greatest human need is belonging. Change that ignores belonging violates the human operating system.

Belonging requires acknowledgment, a simple, human recognition that says: *I see you. I hear you. You matter here.*

Without that acknowledgment, change becomes trauma disguised as progress.

When change has a face, everything shifts. People lean in. They ask questions. They even challenge decisions, not out of defiance but out of trust that their voices will be heard. A visible leader does not hide behind announcements. They communicate early, even when details are not finalized. They share uncertainty with honesty rather than waiting for perfection.

In leadership theory, this is transformational leadership, the ability to inspire action through authenticity. Transformational leaders do not just manage change; they model it. They admit, "I don't have all the answers yet, but I promise to be transparent as we move forward." That single statement diffuses fear faster than any strategic memo ever could.

When change has a face, the process stops feeling like an external force and begins to feel like a shared journey.

Brené Brown defines vulnerability as "having the courage to show up and be seen when we have no control over the outcome." That is what it means to give change a face. It is not about having all the solutions; it is about being willing to stand in the tension between what is known and what is not. Leaders who dare to be seen transform fear into trust. Their openness signals safety, even in the face of uncertainty. Their visibility gives shape to the invisible.

When people can attach a face to someone who listens, explains, and empathizes, they regain their footing. Because what people fear most is not change itself but the loss of connection that often accompanies it.

Part II: The Human Cost of Invisibility

Faceless change always extracts a price. It may manifest as disengagement on a team, distrust within a community, or exhaustion in a family. What begins as an operational decision becomes an emotional wound. In psychology, trauma is not defined by the event itself but by the absence of support after it. The same holds true for organizational trauma.

People can handle layoffs, restructuring, or new leadership if they feel guided through it. But when the process happens to them rather than with them, it leaves a scar that strategy alone cannot heal.

Faceless change replaces belonging with bureaucracy. The faces that once animated the culture fade behind official statements and talking points. The unspoken message becomes clear: your story no longer matters.

Belonging thrives on visibility. Every time a person is invited into a conversation, given context, or asked for input, the system whispers, *you belong here.* Every time communication happens without them, it screams the opposite.

Leaders often underestimate this psychological toll because it does not appear on spreadsheets. But you can feel it in the air, a heaviness that no motivational speech can lift. Productivity slows. Creativity shrinks. Trust erodes grain by grain. Culture does not collapse in a single moment; it dissolves quietly, in the absence of face and voice.

When change loses its face, its consequences multiply downstream. A manager who feels excluded from decisions withdraws from their team. That team disengages from their peers. Departments become silos. The organization fractures, not through conflict but through quiet distance.

Sociologists refer to this phenomenon as *social contagion,* the way emotions and behaviors spread through networks like invisible threads. One person's cynicism becomes another's disillusionment. In a matter of months, what begins as a structural change turns into a cultural crisis. Yet the same principle works in reverse. When leaders restore visibility by communicating openly, admitting mistakes, and involving people, hope becomes contagious too. One act of transparency can reverse months of doubt. Leadership presence is not a soft skill; it is a stabilizing force.

Faceless change is a symptom of systems that value speed over connection. Modern organizations run on data, dashboards, and deadlines. Efficiency is praised as a virtue. But efficiency without empathy is like architecture without a foundation, impressive until the first storm. To restore humanity, leaders must reimagine what progress means. Progress is not just moving forward; it is moving together.

Three practices bring humanity back into change: listening, storytelling, and pacing.

Authentic listening is not waiting to respond; it is being willing to be changed by what you hear. During transitions, people need space to voice uncertainty without fear of punishment. When leaders truly listen, they send a message: *You are part of this process.* Listening turns anxiety into alignment.

Facts inform, but stories transform. Data tells us what is changing; stories tell us why it matters. Neuroscience shows that the brain releases oxytocin in response to authentic stories, fostering trust and empathy. When leaders share stories of struggle, growth, or lessons learned, they humanize the abstract and give change a heartbeat.

Speed often signals control, not competence. Real transformation requires rhythm, action followed by reflection, progress balanced with pause. Pacing allows people to absorb meaning before moving again. When leaders rush, they leave people behind. When they pace with purpose, they bring people along.

Every significant change eventually holds up a mirror to us. It asks not only what we are doing but who we are becoming. Faceless change avoids that mirror. It moves so quickly that no one has time to confront the reflection. Meaningful transformation, however, requires the courage to look and to see what is being gained and what is being lost.

In leadership coaching, this is called *conscious transition.* It is the practice of pausing to ask:

⇒ What values are we protecting?

⇒ What fears are we avoiding?

⇒ Who might be left unseen in this process?

The mirror moment is uncomfortable because it exposes vulnerability. But vulnerability is the birthplace of trust. Brené Brown reminds us, "You cannot get to courage without walking through vulnerability." Leaders who skip reflection in favor of speed trade long-term resilience for short-term relief. The mirror forces honesty, not only about results but about relationships.

Accountability gives change its moral structure. Without it, progress becomes performance.

A faceless leader often hides behind committees or consultants. Decisions are made collectively so that no one can be held responsible. Yet accountability is not about blame; it is about ownership with integrity. When a leader stands before their people and says, "This decision was mine, and here's why," something profound happens. Even those who disagree feel respect. They may not like the outcome, but they trust the process because it is visible. Accountability transforms suspicion into respect.

Simon Sinek describes trust as "a biological reaction to the belief that someone has our best interest at heart." Accountability creates that belief. It is the visible promise that leadership and humanity still share the same space.

Restoring face to change is not only the leader's work; it is cultural work. Presence must be woven into an organization's DNA, from meetings and performance reviews to onboarding and even farewells.

A culture of presence says:

⇒ We speak to people, not about them.

⇒ We make decisions with those affected, not for them.

⇒ We value conversation over convenience.

When this culture takes root, change no longer feels imposed; it feels shared.

Presence also applies to personal life. Families, friendships, and communities face their own transitions as children grow, careers shift, and identities evolve. The same principle applies when change lacks presence, it breeds distance. When it gains presence, it strengthens connection. The smallest acts of conversation, a word of acknowledgment, or a shared silence become the face of care.

Never has humanity been more connected and yet more faceless. Emails replace eye contact. Messages replace meaning. Automation promises convenience but steals communion. Technology is not the enemy; disconnection is.

The challenge for modern leaders is to make digital change human again. This means writing messages that sound like they come from a person, not a program. It means turning cameras on during virtual meetings, using names instead of job titles, and remembering birthdays and stories. The future will only become more automated. The question is whether our leadership will become human alongside it.

Every click, every post, every algorithm represents a choice, to hide or to reveal, to depersonalize or to humanize. The leaders of tomorrow will be those who choose visibility. Metrics matter because they keep organizations accountable, but numbers without narrative flatten humanity.

When success is measured only by profit, output, or performance, people become resources rather than relationships. Yet when metrics are paired with meaning, when each figure is tied to a story, change feels alive again.

Consider a company tracking employee retention. The data shows that 85 percent stayed. The story might reveal that 15 percent left because they felt unseen. The number informs, but the story transforms.

Re-humanizing metrics means asking not only *What did we achieve?* but also *Who did we affect?* Progress without reflection is just motion. Empathy without clarity leads to confusion. Clarity without empathy leads to cruelty. Effective change requires both.

Clarity is a kindness. It reduces the anxiety born from guessing. It respects people enough to tell them the truth, even when it is hard. Leaders often fear that honesty will create panic. The opposite is true. Uncertainty breeds panic; clarity breeds calm.

To give change a face, clarity must be visible in communication, in expectations, and in follow-through. People do not expect perfection; they expect presence.

Every meaningful transformation begins with not knowing. The leaders who thrive are not those who control uncertainty but those who navigate it with authenticity. The most powerful phrase a leader can say during change is, "I don't know yet, but I'm committed to finding out with you." That statement transforms isolation into inclusion. It tells people they are not passengers on a journey; they are partners in discovery.

Leadership, at its core, is not about knowing the way; it is about showing the way. It is about walking the way together.

Beneath every system, structure, and strategy lies something more ancient, the human spirit's need to be seen. When change has no face, that spirit becomes restless. It asks, *where do I belong in this new story?*

Throughout history, societies have marked transitions with rituals: births, marriages, seasons, and endings. Rituals give shape to change; they provide a moment for recognition. Yet in modern life, many of our transitions occur without witnesses. We move from one role to another, one job to the next, one identity to a new one, and rarely pause to honor what is being left behind. Faceless change is change without ritual. It forgets that transformation requires meaning as much as motion.

Leaders, too, need rituals, not religiously, but relationally. They can create space for reflection before launching a new initiative, for gratitude when closing a chapter, and for empathy when people must let go. These pauses remind everyone involved that progress is personal.

There is something sacred about acknowledgment. It tells the human soul, *you mattered here.* Without that acknowledgment, people drift. They carry invisible grief into new beginnings, unable to fully invest because part of them is still holding on to what was.

The antidote is genuine presence, not performance. Presence says, *I see you. I honor this moment. I will walk beside you through what comes next.*

The Loss of Meaning in the Speed of Progress

Modern culture confuses speed with significance. We celebrate the launch, not the learning; the pivot, not the pause. In that constant acceleration, meaning becomes the first casualty. Faceless change thrives in environments obsessed with momentum. Meetings turn into checkboxes. Communication becomes transactional. The "why" behind decisions disappears beneath deadlines.

Meaning, however, sustains people through uncertainty. When individuals understand the purpose of change, they can connect their personal values to the collective vision and gain resilience. They can endure discomfort because it has direction.

Leaders who neglect meaning may win compliance, but they never earn commitment. To restore meaning, slow down. Ask people what the change means to them. Invite stories. Let the room breathe before the next slide. Meaning cannot be manufactured; it must be made together.

How do we reclaim the face of change? How do we return humanity to transformation? It begins with courageous presence, the willingness to be seen even when the outcome is uncertain. The next step is intentional connection, ensuring that every process includes dialogue, representation, and compassion.

Below are guiding principles that turn faceless change into human-centered transformation.

1. Lead with Transparency
People do not need perfect answers; they need honest ones. Transparency replaces rumors with reality. When leaders communicate early, admit their limitations, and explain the reasoning behind their actions, they signal respect. Transparency is not oversharing; it is honoring trust through truth.

2. Center Empathy
Empathy does not weaken leadership; it strengthens it. It reminds people that decisions have human consequences. Before implementing change, pause and ask:

⇒ Who will this affect emotionally?

⇒ What fears might they have?

⇒ How can we honor their dignity through the process?

Empathy bridges what information alone cannot reach the human heart.

3. Model Vulnerability

When leaders admit uncertainty, they invite collaboration. Vulnerability creates psychological safety, the shared belief that it is safe to speak up, make mistakes, and learn. In times of change, safety breeds creativity, creativity fuels adaptability, and adaptability sustains progress. A leader who says, "I am figuring this out too," transforms hierarchy into humanity.

4. Build Belonging

Belonging is the invisible infrastructure of change. Without it, systems crumble no matter how efficient the plan. Build belonging by celebrating diverse perspectives, inviting voices from every level, and publicly recognizing contributions. When people feel part of the change, they protect it.

5. Honor the Past While Building the Future

Faceless change often erases what came before. Human-centered change integrates it. Before closing a chapter, take time to name the successes, lessons, and people who made them possible. Gratitude gives endings grace and offers beginnings legitimacy. You cannot build a future on unacknowledged history.

6. Create Two-Way Feedback Loops

Change without listening is directionless. Invite feedback before, during, and after transformation. Create spaces for surveys, listening sessions, and informal check-ins where people can speak candidly without fear of retribution. Listening is not about control; it is about calibration. The best strategies evolve through conversation.

7. Celebrate Faces, Not Just Metrics

Every transformation rest on human shoulders. Recognize those shoulders. Celebrate the people who made progress possible, not only leaders but also the quiet contributors who turned ideas into reality. Recognition restores humanity to systems that too often forget it. A simple "thank you" can close emotional distance faster than a hundred meetings.

From Faceless to Fearless

When change has no face, it breeds fear. When it gains one, it breeds courage. Fear isolates; courage connects. Fear asks, what if this fails? Courage asks, what if we grow?

The transformation from faceless to fearless begins the moment someone chooses to step forward and be visible. It might be a leader addressing their team, a community organizer, a teacher, or a parent. The title does not matter; what matters is the willingness to be seen.

Every visible act of empathy becomes an anchor in turbulent times. It reminds others that people, not just policies or algorithms, are steering the ship. Visibility becomes not only a leadership strategy but an act of collective healing.

Leadership as Human Witnessing

Leadership, at its essence, is about witnessing humanity as people navigate uncertainty and standing beside them as they rise and fall. The best leaders combine clarity of direction with compassion of presence. They do not hide behind authority; they walk within it, using their influence to amplify others rather than overshadow them.

To witness is to dignify. It is to say, "I see your effort, your confusion, your hope, and I'm still here." When people feel witnessed, they find strength and rediscover purpose. In that rediscovery, change becomes not just tolerable but transformational.

The Return of Meaning

At its highest form, leadership is meaning-making. It connects what is changing with why it matters. Meaning is the antidote to facelessness. It restores the heartbeat to systems and ensures that transformation, no matter how complex, remains grounded in humanity.

When people understand the deeper "why," they internalize the mission. The change becomes personal. It stops being the organization's transformation and becomes our transformation.

Meaning turns compliance into commitment, exhaustion into enthusiasm, and isolation into purpose. Every change, whether organizational, societal, or personal, ultimately reflects on us. It shows the cost and the gain. It asks the timeless question: Who have we become?

If we emerge more efficient but less compassionate, more advanced but less connected, progress was incomplete. If we emerge more transparent, more trusting, and more aware of one another's humanity, change has done its true work.

The mirror does not measure metrics; it measures maturity.

Change is not the enemy of stability; it is the expression of life itself. But without a face, it loses its soul. Faceless change is efficient but empty. It moves systems yet leaves people standing still. When change takes on a face, carried by courage, vulnerability, and voice, it becomes a story worth believing in.

Ultimately, leadership is not about managing change; it is about embodying it. It is about standing where uncertainty meets hope and saying, follow me, I will walk with you. The work of the future is not to eliminate change but to humanize it, to give it faces, names, stories, and meaning.

In every organization, every movement, every relationship, and every life, change without a face becomes fear, but change with a face becomes faith.

Leadership Reflection Prompts

1. **Visibility Check:**

Where in your organization or personal life has change become faceless? Who needs to see your presence more clearly?

2. **Empathy Audit:**

Before your next change initiative, ask: Who will feel this most deeply? How can you include them early?

3. **Story Reclamation:**

What stories are being lost in the pursuit of progress? How might honoring them make the change more meaningful?

4. **Mirror Moment:**

What part of yourself have you outgrown, and have you paused to acknowledge the new version that is emerging?

5. **Human First Principle:**

If every decision were made with the question, "How will this affect people's sense of belonging?" how would your leadership look different?

2

GIVING CHANGE A FACE

Change rarely announces itself with clarity. More often, it arrives quietly: a shift in tone during a meeting, a new policy whispered before it is published, a subtle uncertainty no one dares name.

In one small organization, that is precisely how it began.

A staff of twenty had worked together for years. They knew each other's habits, favorite snacks, and even the sound of each other's footsteps in the hallway. Then one morning, a memo arrived: *Leadership transition effective immediately.*

The director was gone. No explanation. No goodbye.

By noon, rumors replaced facts. By the end of the week, the energy had changed. Smiles faded. Laughter quieted. Meetings filled with tension. No one knew what was happening, but everyone felt it.

Until one Friday afternoon, a mid-level manager named Marcus called the team together. She stood in the middle of the breakroom, holding his coffee cup with both hands.

"I do not have all the answers," he said, his voice shaking slightly. "But I know one thing. We still have each other, and we still have a mission. Until we get more clarity, I will do my best to listen, to keep you informed, and to make sure no one feels left in the dark."

That was it. No grand plan. No polished statement. Just honesty.

Something shifted. The silence that had hung over the office broke. People started talking again, checking on each other, even laughing a little. They did not suddenly know the future, but they had a face to look toward, someone visible, human, and steady.

Marcus did not become the boss; he became the bridge. And in that moment, the team began to heal.

That is the power of giving change a face.

To give change a face is to humanize transition. It is to bring presence to uncertainty, empathy to process, and courage to communication. It does not mean having all the answers. It means standing in the space between the known and the unknown with enough humility to say, *I will walk through this with you.*

Titles do not define leaders who give change a face. They are defined by visibility. They understand that people do not connect to institutions; they connect to people.

When change gains a face, it gains direction. When it loses one, it loses trust.

The human brain is wired to respond to faces. Neuroscientists have found that we can recognize familiar faces faster than any other visual cue, even faster than words. Faces signal safety or threat, belonging or exclusion. They communicate emotion more quickly than language can.

This is why invisible leadership fails. When people cannot see who is leading the change, their instincts interpret it as danger. Their bodies tense. Their trust wavers. But a real, human, imperfect face restores a sense of safety. It tells the body; *you are not alone in this.*

Brené Brown defines courage as "the willingness to show up and be seen when we have no control over the outcome." That is what giving change a face requires, not certainty but presence.

When leaders try to appear flawless, they distance themselves from the very people they are trying to lead. Perfection creates separation, while authenticity creates connection. The leaders who make the deepest impact are not the ones who never falter. They are the ones who admit when they do. They build cultures where questions are safe and vulnerability is not a liability.

In one educational setting, a principal began each semester with a staff meeting where she read aloud her own list of "things I do not yet know how to do." Teachers would laugh, then add their own. The exercise became a ritual not of incompetence but of courage. When we allow others to see our learning, we give them permission to keep growing too.

Visibility is not about spotlighting the self. It is about illuminating the path for others.

Leadership is not a role. It is a relationship. To give change a face, leaders must understand that their presence is a form of communication. Every gesture, tone, and silence sends a message. People notice how you walk into the room, how you respond to pressure, and how you recover from mistakes.

In times of change, people read the *leader* more than they read the *plan*.

When a leader panics, others amplify it. When a leader steadies themselves, others find balance. When a leader listens deeply, others begin to speak honestly.

Giving change a face is, at its core, an act of emotional regulation: choosing to remain calm, compassionate, and grounded even when the ground is shifting beneath you. It is emotional labor, but it is sacred work. Leadership, at its heart, is about creating safety for others as they step into uncertainty.

Empathy is not agreement; it is understanding. It does not require leaders to fix every problem. It only requires them to witness without judgment. When people feel seen, they become more resilient. When they feel dismissed, they disengage.

Leaders who practice empathy do not absorb everyone's emotions; they *hold space* for them. They do not rush to solutions but stay long enough to truly hear.

Imagine a community center facing funding cuts. Staff members are anxious, clients are angry, and rumors spread fast. A leader who practices empathy does not start with numbers; they start with people. They gather everyone together and say, "I know this uncertainty is hard. I feel it too. Let us talk about what we can control and what we can influence together."

That single moment of shared humanity changes the entire emotional temperature. Empathy is not weakness; it is leadership's strongest muscle. It anchors others when information is scarce.

You cannot give change a face if you are disconnected from your own.

Self-awareness is the foundation of visibility. Leaders who have not looked inward struggle to lead outwardly. They react instead of responding and hide instead of healing.

To give change a face, you must first know your own fears that shadow it, the values that shape it, and the purpose that steadies it. Self-awareness transforms reaction into reflection. It turns power into service.

A visible leader asks themselves daily:

⇒ How am I showing up right now?

⇒ What emotions am I carrying into this space?

⇒ Who needs my calm more than my control?

When leadership becomes a mirror, not a mask, people begin to trust again.

3

THE LEADER'S LENS

I spent most of my thirty-three-year career at sea, where Sailors are expected to be. My leadership experience with great teammates and the success that followed allowed me, a Naval Aviator, to be selected to command a fifteen-billion-dollar, forty-five-thousand-ton national asset: the assault aircraft carrier *USS Belleau Wood (LHA-3)*. This vessel carried more than five thousand Sailors and Marines, thirty-five aircraft, and four amphibious vessels that operated in the well-deck at the stern.

One of my most demanding leadership challenges occurred during my tenure as Commanding Officer of *USS Belleau Wood* during Operations Enduring Freedom and Iraqi Freedom. I faced the monumental task of building a cohesive team capable of executing a one-hundred-million-dollar complex overhaul while preparing the crew for impending combat operations in the Middle East.

The ship had been forward-deployed to Japan for the past ten years, leaving minimal time for maintenance and repair of worn engineering systems and other vital components. The U.S. Navy conducts a highly intrusive two-week inspection of all naval vessels every five years, with no exceptions. Unfortunately,

Belleau Wood was scheduled to undergo this Bureau of Inspection and Survey (INSURV) review in the middle of two combat deployments.

The immense pressure of completing the overhaul and subsequent inspection was a challenge my team and I met head-on. Throughout my career, I had been known as a team builder, someone skilled in managing conflict, leveraging individual talent, and developing others. This challenge would test those skills more than I could have imagined.

I began by recognizing the core issues and quickly initiated a strategic plan that demanded disciplined execution to ensure material readiness, which would lead to combat readiness. I relied on my time-tested philosophy: define the challenges, create a clear plan, articulate expectations, and demand transparency from everyone, regardless of rank.

Next, I empowered my Department Heads and Senior Enlisted leaders. That decision sparked a wave of ownership and enthusiasm throughout the entire ship. Even our embarked Marine Expeditionary Unit, more than two thousand warriors headed to Iraq, became motivated and joined in.

Leading from the front and within the bowels of that massive structure, I watched as a lean, determined, five-thousand-strong team came to life. The result was extraordinary. *Team Belleau Wood* completed the one-hundred-million-dollar overhaul three months ahead of schedule and deployed two months early to support Operation Iraqi Freedom.

Exercise

Describe and discuss your company's existing payroll structure, including bonuses awarded for outstanding performance. Also describe and discuss all employee health coverage and other incentives such as educational assistance.

Being knowledgeable, aware, and conversant in these areas fosters sustained appreciation among those most affected by change.

The same meeting. The same agenda. The same people. Yet

two leaders walked away with entirely different stories.

The first leader saw disengagement. She noticed employees staring at their laptops, whispering in the corners, and showing little enthusiasm for her ideas. She left feeling frustrated and unsupported.

The second leader, quietly observing from the back, saw something different. She saw exhaustion, not apathy. She saw people weighed down by deadlines, not defiance. She noticed small nods of agreement that went unspoken because no one wanted to interrupt authority.

The difference between the two was not competence. It was *lens*.

Leadership is as much about how we see as what we do. The same situation can look like resistance or fatigue, lack of initiative or lack of clarity, depending on the lens through which it is viewed. That is the leader's lens, the invisible filter that colors every decision, conversation, and relationship. It is shaped by experience, emotion, and belief. It determines whether we lead with curiosity or judgment, connection or control.

The most powerful leaders are not those with the clearest vision. They are those willing to clean their *lens*.

In every organization, school, or community, patterns repeat themselves. Decisions are made based on perception rather than data. Leaders assume they are interpreting reality objectively, but in truth, they are viewing it through layers of bias, history, emotion, and expectation.

A lens can magnify or distort. It can bring people into focus or blur their humanity. When leaders fail to examine their lens, they begin to confuse assumption for truth. They might label an employee as "unmotivated" when the real issue is burnout. They might call a colleague "difficult" when what they are really seeing is fear disguised as defensiveness.

Our brains crave shortcuts. Neuroscience shows that humans make unconscious judgments within milliseconds, a survival mechanism that helps us navigate complexity. But in leadership, those shortcuts can cost trust, innovation, and inclusion.

Seeing clearly requires a deliberate pause. It means slowing the mental reflex long enough to ask, "What else could be true?"

That one question transforms leadership. When a leader trades certainty for curiosity, they shift from controlling outcomes to cultivating understanding.

Every lens reflects as much as it reveals. What we see in others often says more about what is unresolved in ourselves. A leader who fears being challenged might see assertive employees as threats. One who values harmony above all might interpret disagreement as disloyalty. Another who hides their own self-doubt may project it as criticism of others.

This is the paradox of perception: we see others through the stories we tell ourselves.

That is why emotional intelligence is not optional; it is essential. The ability to notice our own emotions, name them, and navigate them determines how clearly, we see the world around us. Self-awareness is the lens cleaner of leadership.

Without it, even the most well-intentioned leader begins to operate through smudges of past wounds, ego, pride, or fear. Over time, those distortions shape the culture. Teams start mirroring the leader's blind spots, creating a collective blur that no strategy can fix.

But when a leader dares to face their own reflection and ask, *"What part of this pattern belongs to me?"* clarity returns. The leader's lens, after all, begins within.

A clouded lens not only distorts what leaders see; it distorts how people feel seen. When perception hardens into bias, curiosity dies. And without curiosity, trust fades.

One leader described it this way: "I realized I had stopped seeing my team as people and started seeing them as problems to solve." That realization marked the beginning of change.

When people sense that a leader has stopped *seeing* them, they do not argue; they retreat. They stop offering ideas, taking risks, or showing up fully. The air in the room grows heavy with politeness but empty of passion.

The leader's lens does not just shape outcomes; it shapes the emotional climate. Clear vision creates psychological safety, the kind of environment where people feel free to speak, fail, and grow. Clouded vision creates compliance. People perform, but they no longer believe.

One of the most powerful tools a leader can develop is reframing, the ability to look at a situation from a different angle without denying its reality. When something goes wrong, reframing turns "Who is at fault?" into "What can we learn?" When tension rises, it replaces "They do not care" with "They might be scared." When progress slows, it asks, "What is missing from our understanding?" instead of "Who dropped the ball?"

Reframing does not erase accountability; it deepens it. It shifts leadership from blame to ownership, from judgment to learning.

Consider a teacher struggling with a disruptive student. The default lens might see disobedience. The reframed lens asks, *what unmet need is this behavior communicating?* In that simple shift, punishment becomes possibility.

The same holds true for corporate teams, nonprofits, and families. The leader's ability to reframe determines whether conflict becomes a wedge or a window. Reframing does not mean optimism without realism; it means hope with perspective.

Humility is not self-doubt. It is self-awareness without self-importance. The best leaders hold their perspectives lightly. They understand that their view is informed by experience but also limited by it. They invite others to clean the lens with them.

Humility opens space for collective intelligence. A leader once said, "If the only vision in the room is mine, then the view is too small." That is the essence of the leader's lens: expanding the field of vision so others can see themselves in the picture. Humility transforms leadership from command to conversation, from hierarchy to harmony.

No lens stays clear forever. Even the most self-aware leaders are human. They experience fatigue, frustration, and fear. Over time, those emotions leave residue that clouds perception. Stress narrows the view. Ego distorts it. Burnout dulls it. What once looked like an opportunity begins to look like a threat. What once felt like purpose begins to feel like pressure.

That is the danger of an unexamined lens. It starts to define reality rather than reflect it.

One leader admitted, "I did not realize how much my own exhaustion had become part of the culture. I thought I was pushing people toward excellence. I was pushing them past empathy."

Leaders often underestimate how contagious their inner state is. The lens they carry becomes the lens their team inherits. The work, then, is not to pretend clarity never smudges, but to know how to clean it when it does. Clarity is not certainty; it is presence. It is the willingness to stay curious about what is true right now, not what was true yesterday.

Leaders cultivate clarity through practices that ground them: reflection, feedback, stillness, and honest dialogue.

Reflection turns experience into insight. Journaling, debriefing, or even a quiet walk helps leaders translate emotion into understanding.

Feedback acts as an external mirror. Asking "What am I missing?" invites others to help polish the lens.

Stillness creates the pause necessary to reset perspective. In silence, leaders hear what noise hides.

Honest dialogue keeps perception tethered to shared reality. When leaders' welcome truth, even uncomfortable truth, they prevent distortion.

The most grounded leaders are not those who see clearly all the time but those who notice quickly when they have stopped seeing clearly.

The Three Lenses of Leadership Framework

Every leader operates through three lenses: Self, Others, and System. When aligned, they create clarity, connection, and purpose. When disconnected, they create distortion.

1. The Lens of Self: Awareness and Accountability

This lens asks: *How do I see myself, and how does that shape how I lead?*

It is about introspection, knowing your triggers, strengths, and blind spots. It means understanding that every judgment of others reflects your own internal dialogue.

Leaders who use this lens well:

⇒ Pause before reacting.

⇒ Own their part in recurring patterns.

⇒ Choose learning over ego.

Mantra: "I cannot change what I will not acknowledge."

When leaders clean the lens of self, they trade perfection for authenticity. Authenticity builds trust faster than perfection ever could.

2. The Lens of Others: Empathy and Connection

This lens asks: *How do I see those I lead: as roles, or as people?*

It calls for emotional intelligence, curiosity, and deep listening. Through this lens, leaders notice tone as much as words and needs as much as performance.

Leaders who use this lens well:

⇒ Listen to understand, not to reply.

⇒ Seek stories, not summaries.

⇒ Believe that every person wants to succeed but may need different conditions to do so.

Mantra: "Everyone has a story that explains their behavior."

When leaders see others clearly, they transform compliance into commitment.

3. The Lens of System: Context and Complexity

This lens asks: *What environment shapes these behaviors?*

It shifts the focus from individual blame to collective responsibility. It helps leaders identify patterns that no single person caused and address root causes rather than symptoms.

Leaders who use this lens well:

> ⇒ Zoom out to see context before making a judgment.

> ⇒ Consider culture, structure, and process when diagnosing problems.

> ⇒ Balance empathy for individuals with accountability for systems.

Mantra: "If I change the system, I change the story."
When this lens is clear, leadership becomes sustainable. Teams feel supported, not scrutinized.

Bringing the Lenses Together

When leaders use all three lenses in harmony, they practice **integrated vision**: seeing themselves with honesty, others with compassion, and systems with wisdom.

This alignment turns leadership from reaction to reflection, from authority to authenticity. It also creates resilience. When one lens fogs, the others can restore clarity.

A leader aware of self-bias can lean on the empathy lens. A leader overwhelmed by emotion can turn to the systems lens for perspective. A leader lost in complexity can return to self-reflection for grounding.

The more balanced the lenses, the more human the leadership.

Leadership is not about looking good; it is about seeing well. A polished image without clarity is still distorted. Authentic leadership is less about being the one in focus and more about helping others see themselves clearly. Vision, then, is a shared act. It is something we build together.

Artists talk about *negative space,* the parts of a painting that are not filled in but give shape to what is. Leadership has negative space too: the pauses between decisions, the listening between words, the humility between victories. Those moments reveal what leaders truly see.

There will always be times when a leader realizes they have been looking through the wrong lens. The courage lies not in defending the view but in adjusting it. It is humbling to admit, *"I was wrong."* It is braver still to say, *"I see differently now."*

The most transformative leaders allow their vision to evolve. They understand that new information, new people, and new realities demand new ways of seeing. Flexibility is not weakness; it is maturity in motion.

To maintain clarity, leaders can build a simple ritual of reflection around the three lenses.

At the end of each week, ask:

Self: What did I learn about my assumptions?

Others: Who did I listen to the least, and why?

System: What patterns am I noticing that need attention?

Write it down. Share it with a mentor. Discuss it with your team.

The ritual is not about evaluation; it is about evolution. When reflection becomes rhythm, clarity becomes culture.

The leader's lens is not fixed glass; it is a living perspective. It changes with every conversation, every failure, and every act of courage. The question is *not whether the lens will blur, but whether* we will notice when it does.

To lead with clarity is to stay awake to self, awake to others, and awake to the systems we shape.

Leadership, at its essence, is stewardship of vision. It is seeing the unseen, naming the unspoken, and reflecting the best of what humanity can be back to itself.

When a leader looks through a clean lens, they do not just see potential; they illuminate it.

Ultimately, leadership is not about commanding attention. It is about creating clarity, one human face, one honest reflection, and one courageous choice at a time.

Reflection Prompts

1. **Self-Lens:** What personal stories or beliefs most often color how you interpret others' behavior?

2. **Others Lens:** Who in your circle might need to be *seen differently*, with more empathy, curiosity, or trust?

3. **System Lens:** What invisible structures, policies, norms, or assumptions shape your culture more than your intentions do?

4. **Clarity Practice:** How do you know when your lens is smudged, and what helps you clean it?

5. **Legacy Question:** When others look through *your lens,* what do you hope they see reflected?

4

UNSEEN DRIVERS OF RESISTANCE

It was supposed to be a routine meeting, a quick announcement about a new policy designed to make workflows more efficient. The leader stood confidently at the front of the room, slides ready and script rehearsed. Ten minutes later, the air felt heavy. Questions came slower than expected. Some faces were blank. Others nodded politely but seemed distant. The presentation ended with quiet applause, but something had shifted: the energy, the trust, and the connection.

Within days, rumors spread. Productivity slowed. Longstanding collaborators grew guarded. What happened was not rebellion or sabotage. It was quiet, rational, human resistance.

The leader had changed a process, but the people felt something deeper had been altered, their rhythm, their voice, their security. Change had touched something sacred, and that invisible wound began to speak, not through confrontation but through withdrawal. This is how resistance often appears: not as a loud *no*, but as a quiet pause, the breath people take when they are unsure if they still belong in the story being written.

Most leaders' mistake resistance for defiance. They see it as an obstacle to overcome rather than a message to interpret. Yet resistance is rarely about the change itself. It is about the meaning people attach to it. A new system may symbolize loss of control. A new leader may represent an old wound. A reorganization might trigger memories of instability.

Every act of resistance carries a story that began long before the change was announced. When leaders learn to see resistance as data rather than defiance, everything shifts. They stop asking, *"How do I make them change?"* and start asking, *"What is this resistance trying to tell me?"*

Resistance is never random. It is communication in disguise.

In human behavior, resistance is the body's way of protecting itself. When change threatens comfort, identity, or belonging, people instinctively defend those parts of themselves. They are not refusing logic; they are defending meaning.

Psychologists call this **homeostasis**, the natural pull toward stability. In organizations, that instinct appears as attachment to the familiar. We often romanticize adaptability, but stability has purpose too. It is how humans maintain coherence in an unpredictable world.

When leaders understand this, they stop labeling resistance as bad behavior and start recognizing it as a vital clue, a sign that people still care enough to react.

People do not resist change; they resist being changed without meaning. When resistance surfaces, it is rarely about incompetence or disloyalty. It is about protection.

Every change creates emotional geometry, invisible lines connecting hope and fear, loyalty and loss. When a new direction is announced, people do not just evaluate *what* is changing; they feel *what it means* to them personally. For some, it signals opportunity. For others, it signals exclusion.

Even positive change can trigger resistance because it disrupts equilibrium. It forces people to renegotiate their roles, their sense of belonging, and their values.

Resistance, then, is not a sign of failure; it is evidence of impact. It shows that something meaningful has been touched.

When leaders view resistance this way, they approach it not with frustration but with curiosity. They begin to ask deeper questions:

What is this emotion protecting?

What story lies underneath the silence?

What truth have we not yet named aloud?

The Psychology of Resistance

Underneath every act of resistance lies a universal emotion: **fear**.

Not always the dramatic kind, but subtle, lived fear:

Fear of failure

Fear of losing identity or relevance

Fear of being misunderstood

Fear of losing connection to what once felt safe

These fears are often unspoken, even to the person feeling them. They live in tone, body language, and hesitation.

Neuroscience shows that the brain processes social threat the same way it processes physical threat. When people feel excluded or uncertain, their nervous system activates a defensive response.

That is why resistance can seem irrational from the outside, because it is not purely rational. It is biological.

Change asks people to walk into uncertainty, and the brain's primary goal is safety. Without emotional safety, people cannot innovate, create, or adapt. So, when resistance appears, the question is not *"How do I force compliance?"* but *"How do I restore safety?"*

The **vulnerability gap** is the space between *what leaders intend* and *what people experience*. Leaders announce change with confidence, but people receive it through vulnerability. They wonder:

Will I still be needed?

Will I still belong?

Will I still be seen?

This gap widens when leaders skip empathy, when they communicate the plan but not the purpose, the strategy but not the story.

Change without context breeds confusion. Change without compassion breeds resistance.

The most effective leaders do not rush to close this gap with explanation. They bridge it with presence. They stand in uncertainty and say, *"I understand this feels hard. Let us walk through it together."*

That sentence alone can soften an entire room.

Not all resistance is visible. Some of the strongest forms happen quietly, in compliance without commitment.

The employee who attends every meeting but never volunteers ideas

The team that delivers results but no longer brings creativity

The organization that performs well on paper but feels emotionally empty

This is the resistance of disengagement, the kind that hides beneath professionalism.

Invisible resistance is dangerous because it mimics cooperation. It satisfies short-term metrics while eroding long-term trust.

Leaders who want genuine change must learn to sense what is not being said. They must listen for the silence beneath agreement.

When people go quiet, it is not always peace. Sometimes it is surrender.

Silence is data. So is hesitation. So is laughter that no longer reaches the eyes.

The unseen drivers of resistance are not loud. They live in the subtleties of hallway conversations, the energy after meetings, and the turnover that looks voluntary but is not.

To see resistance clearly, leaders must look beyond performance to presence.

Compassion does not eliminate resistance; it transforms it.

When leaders meet pushback with curiosity instead of control, resistance becomes dialogue. When they listen without defensiveness, people begin to trust again.

Genuine compassion is not softness; it is strength guided by empathy. It says, *"I can hold space for your fear without losing sight of our purpose."*

Compassionate leadership is emotional alchemy. It turns fear into feedback, silence into signal, and resistance into relationship.

The next time a team seems uncooperative, a leader might pause and ask, *"What might this resistance be protecting that still matters to them?"*

In that question lies transformation.

Resistance does not live only in people; it lives in systems. Policies, traditions, power structures, and unspoken norms all shape how people respond to change.

The human heart may feel fear, but it is often the system that reinforces it.

A well-intentioned leader once said, "I cannot figure out why my staff is pushing back; they asked for this change." But when she looked closer, she saw a system built on mistrust. Communication flowed one way, decisions were made behind closed doors, and recognition was rare.

People were not resisting her idea; they were resisting *the history that surrounded it.*

Systems remember what people try to forget. Every unacknowledged layoff, ignored suggestion, or instance of performative inclusion becomes part of an organization's emotional architecture. Over time, that architecture shapes response. Even new initiatives must walk through the ghosts of old ones. Leaders who see only the surface will think resistance begins now. Leaders who look deeper understand that most resistance began years ago.

Culture is more than slogans and value statements; it is the emotional climate of a system. And like any climate, it influences behavior more than rules do. When a culture celebrates speed over reflection, resistance takes the form of burnout. When it prizes hierarchy over honesty, resistance becomes silence. When it rewards compliance over curiosity, resistance becomes disengagement. Culture does not prevent resistance; it channels it. To understand resistance, leaders must ask not only *what people are doing but what the system makes possible.*

If the system does not allow people to express disagreement safely, resistance will manifest indirectly through turnover, gossip, or fatigue. "Systems do not change through slogans; they change through safety."

Safety is the soil from which trust grows, and without it, even the best strategies fail to take root. Organizations often tell one story but live another. They say they value transparency while rewarding secrecy, or they promise empowerment while punishing dissent. This gap between intention and experience, between what leaders say and what systems do, breeds resistance faster than any external threat.

People do not resist because they dislike the vision; they resist because the system contradicts it. One educational district launched a "collaborative reform" initiative. The language was inspiring, but teachers were not invited into the design process. When the rollout failed, leadership called it "teacher resistance." In truth, it was *systemic hypocrisy*; the method undermined the message. Alignment is not a communications task; it is an integrity task. When systems align with their stated values, resistance diminishes naturally. People do not fear change when they can trust the process that delivers it.

Resistance is not random. Beneath every slowdown, hesitation, or pushback lie patterns of emotional and systemic forces that influence behavior. Through observation and research, five invisible drivers consistently emerge: *Fear, Fatigue, Loss, Misalignment, and Mistrust*. Each one represents a different dimension of the human experience during change.

1. Fear: The Protector

Fear is the most primal driver of resistance. It is not weakness; it is instinct. In the face of uncertainty, fear asks, *"Will I be safe?"*

That safety can mean physical stability (job security), emotional stability (belonging), or psychological stability (identity). When people do not feel safe, they cling to the familiar, even if it no longer serves them. Leaders often mistake fear for stubbornness. But underneath every "no" lies a "not yet," a request for reassurance. When leaders respond to fear with empathy, it loosens its grip. When they react with pressure, it tightens. Fear is not the enemy; unacknowledged fear is.

Leaders who name fear help neutralize it. "I know this is a big change, and I can see it feels uncertain. Let us walk through what is staying the same." That sentence reactivates trust because it addresses the unspoken question: *"Am I safe here?"*

2. Fatigue: The Silent Saboteur

Not all resistance is emotional. Some of it is simply exhaustion. Change fatigue is real, a physiological and psychological weariness that comes from constant transitions without recovery. People are expected to adapt faster than they can process. One manager called it "initiative overload." Every quarter brought a new strategy, a new slogan, a new tool, and less time to rest. The team was not resistant; they were depleted. Fatigue disguises itself as apathy, but it is really a form of protection. When the mind and body reach their threshold, disengagement becomes a survival strategy.

To address fatigue, leaders must slow down to move forward. They must create rhythms of reflection and recognition, moments when teams can pause, process, and celebrate progress before starting again. "Rest is not a reward for change; it is a requirement for it." Leaders who honor recovery build resilience. Those who ignore it breed resistance.

3. Loss: The Unspoken Grief

Every change brings loss, even positive ones. When people lose a familiar process, a known colleague, or a sense of mastery, they grieve, often silently, because workplaces rarely make space for mourning.

Grief hides behind nostalgia ("It used to be better"), sarcasm ("Here we go again"), or cynicism ("This won't last"). These are not negative attitudes; they are coping mechanisms. When leaders rush people through loss, they confuse speed with progress. The change might be implemented, but hearts remain behind.

Healthy organizations create rituals of recognition, moments to honor what is ending before celebrating what is beginning. A short pause to acknowledge contributions, a thank you for what came before, or even a simple "We know this is hard" can transform loss into loyalty. Change without closure breeds ghosts.

4. Misalignment: The Internal Disagreement

Misalignment happens when people's personal values or lived experiences do not match the organization's new direction. Sometimes, resistance is a sign of integrity, a way of saying, *"I cannot authentically support this because it conflicts with what I believe."*

Leaders often misinterpret this as defiance, but misalignment invites dialogue. It helps reveal ethical blind spots, mixed messaging, or inequities within the system.

At one nonprofit, a new data-tracking policy conflicted with frontline staff's values regarding client dignity. Instead of labeling their hesitation as "resistance," the director asked, "What about this process feels misaligned with our mission?" That conversation led to a redesign that honored both integrity and accountability.

Misalignment, when approached with openness, becomes a compass pointing leaders back toward purpose. "Resistance does not always mean people are wrong; sometimes it means they are right too soon."

5. Mistrust: The Residue of History

The final driver is the most pervasive and the most difficult to heal: mistrust. When people have experienced broken promises or inconsistent leadership, they develop what psychologists call *anticipatory betrayal,* the expectation that change will hurt them again.

This mistrust lingers even when current leaders are sincere. It is the residue of past wounds, embedded in the system's emotional memory. You cannot talk people out of mistrust; you must behave your way out of it. Trust rebuilds slowly, through consistency and care. Leaders must align their words and actions repeatedly until people stop waiting for the other shoe to drop. When mistrust fades, energy returns. People stop resisting not because they have been convinced, but because they feel safe to believe again.

These five drivers rarely exist in isolation. They overlap like weather systems: fear feeds mistrust, fatigue amplifies loss, and misalignment deepens fatigue. When multiple drivers converge, resistance intensifies. But when leaders identify the dominant one, they can address the root cause rather than fight the symptom.

Each driver holds a mirror:

Fear asks for safety.

Fatigue asks for rest.

Loss asks for acknowledgment.

Misalignment asks for integrity.

Mistrust asks for consistency.

The work of leadership is to meet those needs before they harden into opposition. Every leader faces the moment when resistance becomes personal. The frustration builds, the doubt creeps in, and the temptation to push harder grows stronger. But the wisest leaders learn a truth that changes everything: resistance is not an enemy to be conquered; it is an insight waiting to be understood.

When leaders approach resistance with curiosity rather than control, they uncover valuable insights into their people, their culture, and themselves. Resistance, after all, is simply feedback that has not yet been heard.

In times of change, listening is leadership. Not passive listening, but active, courageous listening. Listening to resistance means staying present long enough to hear what is underneath the surface. It means asking questions that invite honesty rather than compliance:

"What is feeling unclear or uncertain right now?"

"What are we afraid we might lose in this change?"

"What do you need from me to feel more supported?"

Leaders who ask these questions are not seeking comfort; they are seeking truth. Often, what emerges is not rebellion but pain. People share stories of past experiences, broken trust, or fear of invisibility. Those stories do not weaken leadership; they humanize it. When a leader can hold another person's truth without defensiveness, the relationship begins to heal.

"Leaders who listen to resistance build the kind of trust no speech could ever create."

Changes made *to* people will always meet resistance.
Change made *with* people transforms resistance into partnership.

Co-creation is the antidote to fear and fatigue. It invites those affected by change to participate in shaping it. It honors autonomy and restores agency. When people help design the future, they stop defending the past.

One community organization found success by shifting from top-down planning to open "listening sessions." They invited members to share not just what they disliked, but what they dreamed. By the end, what began as tension turned into innovation. Co-creation does not slow progress; it strengthens it. Ownership breeds energy, and inclusion builds endurance.

Modern leadership culture often glorifies speed. But in change, speed without understanding is sabotage. Real progress sometimes means pausing long enough for people to make sense of what is happening to let them catch up emotionally with what has already been decided operationally.

One executive reflected, "I used to think slowing down was wasting time. Now I realize it is the only way to make time matter." The paradox of change is that the faster we move, the more resistance we create. The slower we listen, the quicker trust returns.

"When leaders make time for understanding, change starts to feel like belonging."

Emotional accuracy is the ability to recognize which emotion is driving behavior both in others and in oneself. A frustrated team member might not be "difficult"; they might be grieving a loss. A silent employee might not be disengaged; they might be exhausted.

Leaders who cultivate emotional accuracy lead with empathy instead of ego. They know how to name what is real without judgment:

"It sounds like there is some grief here."

"It feels like we are carrying a lot of fatigue right now."

"I sense some mistrust lingering from before. Let us talk about it."
Naming emotions does not create weakness. It creates alignment.
What we can name, we can navigate.

The Reflective Framework: The Five Hidden Drivers

At the heart of this chapter is a framework for recognizing,
interpreting, and responding to resistance not as obstruction but as
opportunity. Each of the five drivers tells a story, and every story
offers a mirror.

Driver	Core Emotion	What It is Protecting	Leadership Response
Fear	Uncertainty	Safety	Provide clarity, reassurance, and honesty.
Fatigue	Overwhelm	Energy	Create rest cycles, reflection, and recognition.
Loss	Grief	Identity	Acknowledge endings and honor transitions.

Driver	Core Emotion	What It is Protecting	Leadership Response
Misalignment	Conflict	Integrity	Engage in dialogue and recalibrate shared values.
Mistrust	Skepticism	Security	Rebuild through consistent action and transparency.

When leaders learn to recognize these drivers, they gain diagnostic insight. Resistance stops feeling mysterious and starts feeling meaningful. The goal is not to eliminate resistance but to interpret it.

At its core, resistance is relational. It reflects the tension between change and connection, between a system's goals and the human need for stability. When people resist, they are protecting their sense of belonging. When leaders respond with presence instead of pressure, resistance softens into relationship.

Every "no" becomes a doorway to understanding. Every hesitation becomes a conversation. Every delay becomes data. The leaders who thrive in uncertain times are those who no longer fear resistance, they befriend it. Because resistance, when met with compassion, reveals not weakness in people but wisdom in systems.

Change asks a great deal from leaders: patience, empathy, and an unshakable sense of purpose. But perhaps the most essential quality is *self-awareness*.

Before addressing others' resistance, leaders must ask:

What part of this discomfort belongs to me?

What fear of my own might be shaping how I interpret theirs?

Am I leading from clarity or from control?

Self-awareness turns frustration into humility. It reminds leaders that resistance is not always external; sometimes it is mirrored within. When a leader dares to look inward, the energy of the entire system begins to shift.

When fear is seen, it becomes courage.
When fatigue is named, it becomes rest.
When loss is honored, it becomes legacy.
When misalignment is explored, clarity emerges.
When mistrust is acknowledged, healing begins.

Resistance, then, is not the opposite of progress, it is part of it. It is the voice of the system asking for balance, the whisper of humanity reminding us that change must move at the speed of trust. Change that honors resistance becomes transformation that lasts.

Leadership in times of change is not about eliminating resistance. It is about creating the emotional and structural safety for resistance to evolve. It is about helping people feel seen, heard, and valued even as they step into uncertainty. It is about recognizing that progress without empathy becomes loss, and empathy without progress becomes paralysis.

Accurate leadership balances both: movement and meaning. Because leadership is not about convincing people to change, it is about *becoming the kind of person they trust to change with.*

Reflection Prompts

1. Which of the five drivers (fear, fatigue, loss, misalignment, mistrust) most often appears in your team or organization, and why?

2. When you encounter resistance, how do you typically react? What would curiosity look like instead?

3. Where in your leadership have you mistaken compliance for commitment?

4. What stories or histories might be shaping resistance that you have not yet acknowledged?

5. How can you build rest, recognition, and reflection into your next change effort?

5

CULTURE: THE INVISIBLE FACE OF THE ORGANIZATION

T he first effective leader whose image remains etched in my mind is my maternal great-grandfather. He was a proud World War I veteran (cook), a hardworking sharecropper in the low country of Allendale, South Carolina, and most importantly, the devoted father of fifteen children in a blended family.

By God's providence, I was raised by him and my great-grandmother. I was even delivered by a midwife in their home. On that small, rural farm of sandy soil, I watched this disciplined man, the CEO of the Holmes family enterprise, rise every day at 5 a.m. to meet the countless demands that defined both farm and family life.

As a loving father, he disciplined with equal measures of love, firmness, and flexibility. As a businessman in the segregated South, he understood how to build relationships that turned competition into collaboration. Under his guidance, a community of poor farmers with limited tools accomplished far more together than they ever could alone. He often said, "Teamwork makes the dream work."

These simple yet profound lessons from a man with only a third-grade education lie at the core of my understanding of effective leadership.

They shaped how I led as a high school section leader for four years, as a college coordinator overseeing more than seventy tutors under the chancellor, as a church elder and youth ministry leader for seven years, and as a naval officer commanding operations that spanned over 600,000 nautical miles.

Yes, teamwork does make the dream work. But just as vital to effective leadership is the leader's internal world, their personality, awareness, and emotional intelligence. Leaders must cultivate mental and emotional tools that help them ignite creativity and innovation, especially among those who think and process differently.

In the following chapters, I will introduce five essential awareness traits I call *"The Essential Self-Awareness Traits of an Effective Leader."*

The Essential Self-Awareness Traits of an Effective Leader:

1. Inner Self-Awareness

2. Awareness of the Needs of Those Around You

3. Awareness of the Power of Silence

4. Awareness of One's Shadow (and how to avoid acting it out inappropriately)

5. Awareness Not to Take Yourself Too Seriously

A deep consciousness of these five dimensions can transform relationships, especially professional ones. These awarenesses may, in fact, prove more valuable than any credential or certification a leader holds.

Throughout my career as a Licensed Clinical Behavior Modifier and Marriage and Family Therapist in the U.S. Navy, I have been deeply influenced by the work of Swiss psychiatrist Carl Jung, founder of analytical psychology. Among his greatest contributions are his theories on the collective unconscious, archetypes, introversion and extroversion, and personality types, which later formed the foundation for the **Myers-Briggs Type Indicator (MBTI).**

Through years of counseling hundreds of active-duty personnel and their families across my command, from Southeast Asia to Iceland, I have come to believe a powerful truth: **we are the sum total of all our experiences, both good and bad.**

Jung also introduced the concept of the **shadow**, the darker, hidden aspects of one's personality that are often suppressed, including both negative traits and unacknowledged potential. Integrating the shadow through self-reflection and acceptance, what Jung called *shadow work*, is essential to emotional balance and authenticity.

What the Shadow Is

The Dark Side: The shadow represents the unconscious part of the psyche that holds qualities we reject, such as selfish desires, insecurity, anger, or cruelty.

Personal vs. Collective: Jung distinguished between the personal shadow, which is unique to each person, and the collective shadow, which represents shared societal biases such as racism or xenophobia.

Hidden Potential: The shadow is not purely negative. It can conceal positive traits like creativity, instinct, and sensitivity that were suppressed out of fear or social pressure.

How the Shadow Manifests

a. *Projection:* When unaware of our shadow, we project it onto others, seeing in them what we refuse to see in ourselves.

b. *Behavioral Symptoms:* It can surface as irritability, sudden moods, or irrational behavior.

c. *Dreams:* The shadow often appears symbolically in unsettling dreams, offering clues about our inner life.

The Importance of Shadow Work

a. *Confronting and Accepting:* Shadow work is not about erasing darkness but acknowledging and integrating it.

b. *Achieving Wholeness:* Through this process, individuals access hidden strengths and become more balanced and self-aware.

c. *Growth and Healing:* It reduces projection, fosters empathy, and strengthens relationships.

d. *Individuation:* Integration of the shadow is key to what Jung called individuation, the process of becoming a fully realized person.

This psychological framework aligns deeply with my Christian faith. I believe that all life experiences, no matter how painful, have meaning and developmental value. The Apostle Paul expressed this truth in Romans 8:28:

"And we know that in all things God works for the good of those who love Him, who have been called according to His purpose."

To me, this verse provides both spiritual and psychological insight. It helps reconcile suffering and purpose, giving foundation to Jung's observations. If the unconscious truly stores our unprocessed experiences, then what remains unexplored can subtly control our choices, shaping our reality in ways we do not recognize.

Self-awareness, therefore, is not optional; it is everything. The more you know, the more you grow. As Jung said, *"Who looks outside, dreams; who looks inside, awakes."* He also wrote, *"Until you make the unconscious conscious, it will direct your life and you will call it fate."*

Other Jungian insights include:

1. "Your vision will become clear only when you can look into your own heart. Without, everything seems discordant; only within does it coalesce into unity."

2. "The privilege of a lifetime is to become who you truly are."

3. "The most terrifying thing is to accept oneself completely."

"Everything that irritates us about others can lead us to an understanding of ourselves."

These truths reveal that confronting one's inner life is the only way to achieve authentic leadership and conscious living. The journey toward self-awareness is the journey toward wholeness, and the foundation of a culture where leadership becomes not just positional, but deeply personal.

As we move toward unpacking my five Essential Self-Awareness Traits of an Effective Leader, I want to provide additional insights into why this process of inner reflection is essential to personal and professional growth, especially for those entrusted with leading and influencing others.

Process thinking is a mindset that focuses on the method or sequence of steps to achieve a goal rather than on the outcome alone. It involves breaking down complex tasks into smaller, manageable parts and improving the process through observation, analysis, and feedback. This approach is used in business, education, and professional sports to boost efficiency, identify bottlenecks, and ensure consistent, high-quality results.

Key components of process thinking include:

Deconstructing tasks: Breaking a complex goal into clear, logical steps.

Focusing on the journey: Prioritizing consistent execution over quick results. Success is built through daily discipline.

Continuous improvement: Using feedback to identify inefficiencies and opportunities for refinement.

Systems view: Recognizing how interconnected parts work together within a larger system.

Dynamic adjustment: Adapting and refining processes as contexts change.

Each element requires effective leadership for proper implementation. Because people are central to every system, leaders at all levels must approach this work with openness and humility.

Arbinger Institute's training principle, "change your mindset, change your destination," captures this truth well. It teaches that most organizational and personal problems stem from a self-focused or **inward mindset**. Shifting to an **outward mindset**, one that considers the needs and goals of others, transforms behavior and creates lasting change.

According to Arbinger, every person and organization operates from one of two core perspectives:

Inward Mindset: A self-focused view that prioritizes personal goals while disregarding impact on others. This mindset sees people as:

a. Objects to be used for personal gain

b. Obstacles to be overcome

c. Irrelevancies to be ignored. It leads to blame, conflict, disengagement, and weak collaboration.

Outward Mindset: A perspective that aligns personal goals with the goals of others. It recognizes people as individuals with their own needs and aspirations. This shift encourages:

a) Improved collaboration

b) Greater accountability

c) Increased innovation and engagement

Arbinger's model shows how mindset shapes outcomes through a clear progression:

1. **Mindset:** The lens through which you view the world, either inward or outward, drives your behavior.

2. **Behavior:** Your actions and decisions, guided by mindset, shape your relationships and influence others.

3. **Results:** The outcomes of these behaviors determine your ultimate success or failure in both personal and organizational performance.

The central lesson is this: no matter what system, framework, or professional tool a leader uses, progress depends on awareness and mindset at the top. As the Navy saying goes, the one who gives the rudder orders controls the course and destination of the ship.

The new leader arrived full of energy and vision. Her first week was filled with introductions, tours, and enthusiasm. "This place has great potential," she told her team. "I can feel the energy."

By her third month, that energy had shifted. Projects slowed. Decisions stalled. Meetings filled her calendar, but progress remained elusive. People smiled in public but whispered in private. Every idea received polite agreement and quiet dismissal. When she asked for feedback, no one disagreed openly. They simply said, "That is not how we usually do things."

There were no protests or acts of rebellion, just an invisible resistance. Something unseen but deeply embedded shaped how things got done. It decided who was heard, how risk was measured, and what felt safe. The organization had an identity, not the one printed on its mission statement, but the one quietly living in its hallways.

That unseen identity is what we call **the organization's invisible face**. Every company, no matter how structured or visionary, develops an invisible face, the sum of its emotions, habits, and relationships. This face is not physical; it is cultural. It is the collective personality that greets people before any person does.

When you walk into a workplace, you can feel it:

The energy in the lobby

The tone of hallway conversations

The way people pause before speaking up

The quiet hierarchy that decides whose voice matters

That atmosphere, subtle yet undeniable, is the invisible face. Newcomers sense it before they understand it. Longtime employees stop noticing it because it feels normal. Often, it contradicts the organization's stated values.

A company may call itself "collaborative" yet reward guarded competition. It may celebrate "innovation" but quietly punish failure. It may claim "people are our greatest asset" while ignoring burnout. When what is said and what is felt no longer match, people stop believing the surface story. They start reading the emotional truth. The invisible face becomes the organization's true leader, silent, consistent, and deeply human.

No one designs the invisible face intentionally. It forms over time through thousands of small interactions, habits, and reactions. Every leader contributes to it. Every policy reinforces it. Every silence shapes it. Culture is not written in slogans; it is written in behavior.

The invisible face takes shape when people notice what *happens* in moments of pressure:

Who receives credit and who is forgotten

How dissent is handled

Whether mistakes lead to curiosity or blame

Whether people can say "I don't know" without fear

Each moment adds a brushstroke to the organization's portrait. Over time, people learn its expressions, when to smile, when to stay silent, and when to step back. The culture becomes muscle memory. Even new leaders, once determined to transform it, often end up conforming to it. They start by leading and end by adapting. That is why culture often outlasts leadership. You cannot change what you cannot name.

An organization is more than a structure. It is an emotional ecosystem. Every system carries feelings, not as individuals do, but through the flow of emotion across teams. In meetings, you can sense tension or ease. In emails, urgency or hesitation. In decisions, confidence or fear.

These collective emotions form the blueprint employees follow. When anxiety dominates, people seek safety through silence. When competition rules, people prioritize survival over collaboration. When care and purpose guide the culture, people risk creativity.

The invisible face is the emotional climate made visible through behavior. Leaders who ignore emotion allow it to rule them. Leaders who acknowledge emotion begin to lead it. The invisible face is not about being pleasant; it is about being *aware*. Every organization has two sets of values: the ones it declares and the ones it demonstrates.

The declared values live in posters, websites, and HR manuals. The demonstrated values live in meetings, decisions, and hallway conversations. When those two faces do not align, tension builds.

Employees experience cognitive dissonance, the discomfort of hearing one truth but living another. That dissonance slowly erodes trust. A company may claim "transparency" while leaders share decisions only after they are finalized. A school may preach "collaboration" yet reward individual competition. A nonprofit may highlight "equity" while maintaining homogeneity in its leadership. This is not always hypocrisy; it is human. Every system wrestles with the space between aspiration and action. But when that gap becomes habitual, the invisible face hardens into cynicism. People begin to say, "That's just how things are around here."

The moment those words become normal, innovation dies because the story of inevitability replaces the story of possibility.

The invisible face, if left unnamed, becomes the ceiling of what is possible. Even when people leave, systems retain emotional traces of past experiences such as layoffs, conflicts, successes, betrayals, and leadership changes. These memories live in quiet phrases like

"Last time we tried that" or "That didn't go well before." This collective memory shapes how new ideas are received. It is not that people resist change; it is that they have learned not to trust it.

When culture carries unhealed memory, progress feels like risk. Leaders who overlook this mistake caution for resistance instead of recognizing it as wisdom. Healing an organization's memory does not begin with new goals; it begins with new conversations. It requires acknowledging history aloud, naming what went wrong, and naming what was lost. It invites collective forgiveness not to erase the past, but to release it.

The invisible face cannot be renewed until its history is honored. Before culture can evolve, it must be seen. Before it can be seen, it must be named.

The invisible face is most evident in how belonging is distributed. Every organization, consciously or unconsciously, communicates who fits and who does not. Sometimes it is explicit in hiring patterns or leadership representation. Other times it is subtle, in tone, humor, or who gets invited to informal conversations.

Belonging is not declared; it is experienced.
When people feel they must shrink to fit; the invisible face becomes exclusionary. When they can expand to contribute, it becomes empowering.

Culture is not what leaders say about inclusion; it is what people feel about participation. At its best, the invisible face reflects belonging. At its worst, it reflects hierarchy disguised as harmony.

The work of leadership is to look beyond comfort and ask: *Who isn't visible here, and why?*

Every organization has two cultures, the one people talk about and the one people live. The spoken culture exists in policies, training, and retreats. The lived culture exists in tone, reaction, and rhythm. If you want to know which one is real, pay attention not to what leaders *say*, but to what people *fear*.

Fear reveals truth. It shows what people have learned not to question, not to ask, and not to feel.

In one company, employees described their leader as "the visionary." They admired his intelligence and drive but admitted they rarely spoke up in meetings. "It's just easier," one said. "You don't want to be on his bad side." Publicly, the organization celebrated innovation. Privately, fear governed creativity. The invisible face was not visionary; it was vigilant.

Every organization has that second layer, the *culture beneath the culture*. That hidden layer decides what gets rewarded, tolerated, or punished. It determines whose ideas are safe, how failure is handled, and whether vulnerability is seen as strength or risk.

The real culture is what happens when no one is taking notes.

When leaders learn to observe this hidden layer through silence, body language, and unspoken norms, they begin to see the organization's most authentic self. Culture is rarely taught directly; it is absorbed through imitation.

New employees do not read manuals to learn how things work. They watch how people behave in meetings. They notice who interrupts, who is praised publicly, and whose opinions disappear. They learn when laughter is permitted and when silence is expected. These micro-observations teach belonging more effectively than any orientation session.

Once those cues are internalized, they become self-reinforcing. No one has to enforce the rules because everyone already knows them. That is how invisible culture becomes self-sustaining: it operates through habit, not policy.

The leader's role is not to invent culture, but to reveal it, to make the unspoken speakable. Once visible, it can be reshaped. Until then, it rules quietly, unquestioned.

Leaders often underestimate how much of themselves the organization absorbs. Culture reflects leadership, not only what leaders *do*, but who they *are*. A leader's energy becomes the organization's emotional climate.

If a leader is anxious, urgency spreads. If a leader is defensive, silence multiplies. If a leader is grounded and curious, people breathe easier. This mirroring is not deliberate; it is human. People look to leadership for cues about safety and significance.

In one educational organization, staff described their director as "always on edge." Over time, meetings grew tense, creativity dropped, and even casual conversations became cautious. When the director took a sabbatical, something remarkable happened: people started laughing again. The structure did not change; the atmosphere did.

That moment revealed a truth: leadership is not just a role; it is *emotional architecture*. Every leader builds an atmosphere. Every reaction, tone, and choice adds texture to the invisible face.

This is why self-awareness is not optional; it is the foundation of culture. The organization becomes what the leader repeats. The leader's invisible face eventually becomes the organization's invisible face.

The behaviors leaders tolerate are the ones that multiply. The emotions they model are the ones that echo. If a leader interrupts others, soon everyone does. If a leader admits mistakes, humility becomes safe. If a leader listens deeply, dialogue expands.

This echo effect explains why cultural transformation starts not with mission statements but with mirrors.

It is not about asking, "How do we change the organization?" It is about asking, "What in me is being reflected through this culture?"

When leaders make that shift, change becomes less about control and more about consciousness. Culture mirrors leadership, but leadership must first mirror truth.

Just as individuals have identities, organizations have visible and invisible layers that shape how they function and feel. The visible face lives in strategy, goals, and operations. The invisible face lives in emotion, story, power, and belonging.

To understand that essence, leaders can study the Four Invisible Faces of an Organization: Culture, Narrative, Power, and Belonging. These are not abstract ideas; they are the quiet forces that determine how people behave when no one is watching.

1. Culture: The Face of Habit

Culture is the organization's muscle memory, the habits that outlast policy and personality. It is what people do instinctively, not because they are told to, but because that is how it is done here.

Culture cannot be changed through command. It changes through pattern.

To reshape culture, leaders must first identify its unspoken rules:

What is rewarded most often?

What is ignored without consequence?

What do people apologize for that they should not have to?

What do they tolerate that they secretly resent?

These questions expose culture's wiring. Healthy cultures reward curiosity over control, effort over image, and dialogue over deference. Toxic cultures do the opposite.

Culture is not fixed; it is practiced. And every practice is a choice. Leaders shift the invisible face of culture by modeling new habits until they spread. When consistency replaces contradiction, trust begins to return.

2. Narrative: The Face of Story

Every organization tells a story about itself. Some stories are hopeful: "We make a difference." Some are defensive: "We survive no matter what." Some are heroic: "We are the best." And some are haunted: "We have been burned before."

These narratives function like collective memory. They shape decisions more deeply than data ever can. The story an organization tells itself becomes its truth. When the narrative centers on scarcity, people compete. When it centers on fear, people hide. When it centers on possibility, people innovate.

Leaders do not just communicate stories; they curate them. Every meeting, every acknowledgment, every response to failure either reinforces or rewrites the story.

For example, when a leader responds to a mistake with curiosity rather than punishment, they shift the story from *fear of failure to freedom to learn.* This is narrative leadership, the art of changing culture through story. The invisible face of an organization is the story it tells when no one is listening. When people begin telling a new story, even quietly, transformation has already begun.

When the Story Becomes Stuck

Sometimes the invisible face hardens into an old story that no longer fits the present. Phrases like "We have always done it this way" or "That won't work here" signal a narrative stuck in time. To renew culture, leaders must soften those stories by asking thoughtful questions:

"What if that were no longer true?"

"What story would we rather tell next?"

"What if our best chapter hasn't been written yet?"

When leaders invite people to imagine beyond the old narrative, hope returns. And hope is the foundation of all change.

3. Power: The Face of Access

Power is the least discussed and most decisive feature of any culture. It determines whose voices are amplified, whose ideas are adopted, and whose concerns are quietly dismissed.

Every organization distributes power formally through hierarchy and informally through relationships, reputation, and proximity to leadership. In healthy systems, power circulates like oxygen: it fuels clarity, growth, and inclusion. In unhealthy systems, it stagnates, accumulating in the same rooms and around the same people, reinforcing sameness under the illusion of stability.

Power becomes invisible when it feels normal. People stop questioning who has access to decisions because it seems "natural." Yet what feels natural is often just what is familiar. The real measure of culture is how power moves when no one is watching.

When leaders hold on to control, culture stiffens. When they share it wisely, culture breathes.

The invisible face of power is shaped by three quiet choices:

1. **Whose truth is validated.**

2. **Whose discomfort is tolerated.**

3. **Whose growth is prioritized.**

If the same people are validated, protected, and promoted year after year, the organization's invisible face becomes predictable and exclusive.

True leadership does not mean giving away power recklessly. It means expanding access thoughtfully. It means ensuring that decision-making reflects diversity of thought, background, and perspective. Because when people see themselves in power, they see themselves in possibility.

The Myth of Neutral Systems

No organization is truly neutral. Every policy, process, and practice carries bias, a point of view embedded in its design. When leaders say, "We treat everyone the same," it often means they have not examined who "everyone" was originally built to serve.

Neutrality is often invisibility in disguise. To make an organization equitable, leaders must expose the invisible advantages built into its structure:

Who holds informal influence versus formal authority?

Whose ideas receive second chances?

Whose mistakes are treated as learning, and whose are treated as liability?

These patterns of power define the real rules of engagement. Healthy organizations make those rules visible, not to shame or punish, but to realign. They talk openly about privilege, bias, and decision-making so that power becomes transparent and trust grows.

When power is invisible, it protects comfort. When power is visible, it protects integrity.

4. Belonging: The Face of Safety

If culture is habit, narrative is story, and power is access, belonging is the heartbeat. It determines whether people show up authentically or selectively. It answers the question, "Is it safe to be myself here?"

When belonging thrives, people risk vulnerability. They contribute beyond their roles. They innovate because they feel valued, not just evaluated. But when belonging is absent, performance becomes protection. People hide what is human to appear acceptable.

Leaders often mistake participation for belonging. People can attend meetings without ever feeling included in meaning. Belonging is emotional, not logistical. It is measured not by attendance, but by trust.

You can sense belonging in the small things, the laughter that feels natural, the disagreements that stay respectful, the silence that holds thought instead of fear.

Belonging is not a policy; it is a promise: to see, hear, and honor the whole person.

An organization's invisible face is most visible in who feels safe to speak truth. When people experience belonging, feedback becomes dialogue. When they do not, silence becomes survival.

Exclusion does not always look like discrimination. Sometimes it looks like exhaustion, the quiet fatigue of constantly translating yourself, your ideas, your tone, your presence to fit an invisible norm.

In one research group, an employee said, "I am not excluded. I am just tired of adjusting." That sentence captured the essence of invisible exclusion.

Leaders rarely see this because exclusion often hides beneath performance. People meet goals and complete tasks while carrying invisible emotional labor. To shift the invisible face, leaders must name this labor and invite stories of exclusion, not as accusations, but as acts of truth-telling.

Culture evolves not through policy, but through shared humanity.

The invisible face of an organization is not a puzzle to solve; it is a mirror to hold. The goal is not to erase the invisible but to illuminate it, turning implicit patterns into explicit choices.

That starts with observation:

What emotions fill the room before words do?

What truths are felt but never said?

What values are professed but not practiced?

Leaders who slow down to notice these cues begin to see the full picture. They realize that transformation is not only about what changes, but about what finally becomes visible.

Awareness is the first act of culture change.

The Reflective Framework: The Four Invisible Faces

Invisible Face	What It Represents	Questions for Leaders
Culture	The habits and assumptions that define behavior.	What do we reward, ignore, or excuse without realizing it?
Narrative	The story we tell about who we are.	What story are we repeating and what story do we want to tell next.

Invisible Face	What It Represents	Questions for Leaders
Power	How access, privilege, and influence move through our system.	Who has the microphone and who never gets it?
Belonging	The emotional experience of safety and inclusion.	Who feels seen, and who feels invisible?

These four faces define every organization as the unseen architecture beneath strategy, performance, and policy.

To lead effectively, one must look beyond visible metrics of success and sense the invisible emotions that shape culture. Once the invisible face is recognized, the next step is alignment: ensuring that values, behavior, and structure reflect one another.

Alignment happens when what people experience matches what leaders declare. It is when "how we do things" feels consistent with "why we do them."

To create alignment, leaders can:

1. **Name the Gaps.** Speak honestly about where culture contradicts values.

2. **Model New Patterns.** Demonstrate vulnerability, curiosity, and fairness daily.

3. **Measure What Matters.** Track belonging, trust, and engagement as seriously as profit.

4. **Reward Transparency.** Celebrate truth-telling even when it is uncomfortable.

5. **Revisit the Story.** Reaffirm purpose as the organization evolves.

Alignment is not perfection; it is congruence. When culture, power, and belonging move in harmony, the organization feels alive.

Every time leadership changes, the organization gets a new mirror. Every policy and every shift in tone reshapes the invisible face in subtle ways. The question is never *"Will the face change?"* but *"Will we be intentional about what it becomes?"*

When leaders act with awareness, courage, and compassion, they reshape the invisible face into one that reflects humanity rather than hierarchy. When that happens, people do not just follow, they flourish.

The invisible face of an organization is not built by strategy; it is revealed through relationship.

Leadership Reflection Prompts

1. What part of your organization's invisible face most reflects your own leadership habits?

2. When you walk into a room, what emotion do you think people feel, and what do you want them to feel?

3. Where does your organization's declared culture differ from its lived one?

4. Whose stories or truths are missing from your cultural narrative?

5. What small act could you take this week to make the invisible visible?

The invisible face is not what an organization says it is; it is what it unconsciously shows the world every day. It is the energy in its conversations, the consistency of its actions, and the integrity of its choices.

When leaders dare to see this face clearly, they unlock the possibility of transformation not just in systems but in souls. Because every organization is a living reflection of its people, and every leader has the power to change what it reflects.

6

PITFALLS OF FACELESS LEADERSHIP

Before and after the Iraqi invasion of Kuwait in August 1990, which later escalated into Operation Desert Storm, the Persian Gulf and its oil assets were protected and patrolled by only three naval combatant ships. I had the honor of serving on one of those destroyers. The ship's challenges, and more importantly, the crew's ability to overcome them, were expertly written about by one of its senior department heads, CDR Leo Grassilli, SC, USN.

As the ship's Aviation Department Head, I witnessed firsthand the difficulties the entire crew endured due to a lack of mutual trust and confidence between our two highest-ranking officers. Yet, this tightly knit team, from E-1 to O-5, united and became a combat-ready force in the face of overwhelming odds during the summer of 1990. After multiple Navy aircraft carriers and U.S. Air Force squadrons arrived, we continued our mission through a six-month extended deployment.

The good news is that our commanding officer eventually recognized our many "unforced errors" and grew more effective as we journeyed back to our homeport.

Faceless Red Flags:

Mistrust of subordinates except the Executive Officer

Avoiding crew spaces

No effective "Captain's Calls" to share crucial updates

Ineffective communication up and down the chain of command

Turning Point: When the ship was dead in the water for twelve hours in a hostile combat zone

The auditorium was full. The slides were perfect. The mission was clear. The leader stood center stage, confident, articulate, and charismatic. He spoke about innovation, efficiency, and the organization's bold new future. The words landed beautifully. The applause was polite. But as people left the room, they were not talking about what had been said; they were talking about how they felt—unseen, unheard, and unneeded.

The leader did not notice. He had delivered his message flawlessly. He had presented the vision with conviction, but without connection.

Weeks later, the initiative stalled. Engagement dropped. Creativity faded. He blamed execution. The truth was simpler: the people no longer saw themselves in the story.

This is how faceless leadership begins, not through malice or incompetence, but through distance. When leaders stop seeing people as participants and start seeing them as instruments, the face of leadership begins to fade. "A leader can't inspire what they no longer see."

Most leaders do not wake up one day disconnected. It happens gradually, a thousand small compromises that trade relationship for results:

⇒ A skipped conversation because "there's no time."

⇒ A decision made without input because "it's faster this way."

⇒ A compliment withheld because "they already know they're doing well."

Each omission creates distance. Each layer of distance dulls empathy. Soon, leaders speak in metrics instead of meaning, in goals instead of gratitude. The people listening stop bringing their hearts to work. They offer compliance, not commitment.

Faceless leadership is not cold; it is numb. It is what happens when leaders, overwhelmed by demands, disconnect from their own humanity to stay productive. It is leadership on autopilot, efficient, impressive, and emotionally vacant.

The irony is that faceless leadership often begins with good intentions. Leaders want to protect their teams from chaos, shield them from hard truths, or maintain order during uncertainty. But in doing so, they remove the very thing that makes leadership transformative: presence.

Presence is not about being in the room; it is about being attuned to the room. When leaders stop noticing how people feel, they stop leading and start managing. Disconnection is the first and most insidious pitfall of faceless leadership. It is subtle because it is socially acceptable. You can run an efficient meeting while being emotionally absent. You can deliver quarterly goals while being relationally blind. You can even win awards while losing connection.

Disconnection corrodes trust quietly. It appears not as conflict, but as withdrawal. People stop offering ideas. They start doing just enough. They show up, but not fully.

Leaders often interpret this as laziness or disengagement. It is neither. It is a signal that people have stopped feeling seen. When people feel unseen, they stop caring. And when leaders stop caring, culture stops breathing.

Ask anyone in an organization to describe their leader, and you will hear adjectives like "decisive," "driven," or "visionary." But ask them how their leader makes them *feel*, and you will hear the truth. Do they feel trusted or inspected? Empowered or micromanaged? Appreciated or invisible?

That is the mirror test. Faceless leadership fails not because it lacks skill, but because it lacks reflection. Leaders become so focused on outcomes that they forget the *emotional impact* of their presence. They forget that leadership is not about being the smartest person in the room; it is about being the most human. "People do not need perfect leaders; they need present ones."

At some point, visibility increases. People look up, listen, and depend on their leader. With visibility comes the temptation to curate rather than connect. The leader begins to edit their tone, their opinions, and their vulnerability. They project confidence even when they feel doubt. They perform certainty even when they are unsure. Slowly, authenticity gives way to performance. Leadership becomes an act, and the audience becomes employees.

This is the second stage of faceless leadership, when connection is replaced by presentation.

On the surface, everything looks strong: high engagement scores, polished messages, smooth rollouts. But beneath it all grows quiet hollowness. People can sense performance even when they cannot name it.

Leaders forget that authenticity is contagious, and so is artifice. When leaders pretend, teams perform rather than connect. Faceless leadership thrives in environments that reward control and perfection. Leaders begin to wear competence like armor. That armor protects them from criticism but isolates them from connection. Vulnerability, not authority, builds trust.

When leaders refuse to show uncertainty, they deny others permission to show truth. Teams become performative, meetings rehearsed, and real problems buried. One leader confessed, "I didn't realize my silence was teaching everyone else to hide."

That admission captures the essence of faceless leadership: when the desire to appear strong makes the organization emotionally weak. Real leadership does not come from flawless performance; it comes from honest presence. The face of leadership is not perfection; it is presence.

In modern workplaces, efficiency is idolized. Leaders are praised for speed, decisiveness, and results. But when efficiency becomes obsession, empathy becomes collateral damage. Emails replace conversations. Dashboards replace dialogue. Metrics replace meaning. And somewhere between deadlines and deliverables, the leader's face disappears.

People stop approaching them not out of disrespect, but out of self-protection. Faceless leadership creates functional systems and fractured souls. Everything works, but nothing connects.

People rarely remember efficiency, but they always remember empathy. They remember how leaders made them feel under pressure, not how quickly they checked boxes. Efficiency without empathy may deliver performance, but it never delivers purpose.

When leadership loses its face, organizations lose their soul. Employees adapt by protecting themselves, withholding ideas, and minimizing risks. Innovation suffers because creativity requires vulnerability, and vulnerability requires safety.

At the top, leaders feel lonely. They interpret silence as harmony, busyness as productivity, and compliance as loyalty. Beneath the surface, their teams are emotionally absent. Disconnection becomes mutual. Leaders feel unseen by their people, and people feel unseen by their leaders. Both retreat, each waiting for the other to make the first move.

This cycle does not break with strategy; it breaks with sight. The antidote to faceless leadership is not more communication but more connection. Leaders must learn to see again, not just the numbers, but the faces behind them.

The Ego Trap

Ego is not arrogance; it is insecurity in disguise. It whispers, *"I need to be right to be respected."*

For many leaders, ego begins as a defense mechanism. Years of proving themselves, carrying expectations, and enduring scrutiny make validation feel like survival. Over time, they equate leadership with being the smartest, the most composed, the most indispensable.

But the higher they climb, the more fragile that validation becomes. The applause fades. The feedback becomes filtered. The environment grows polite but distant. So ego builds identity out of image. The title becomes armor; the position becomes proof.

Faceless leadership is not only about losing sight of others; it is about losing sight of self. "When a leader forgets who they are without the title, they lead from ego instead of essence."

Ego thrives on control because control feels like certainty, and certainty feels like safety. But control is a mirage. The tighter leaders hold, the less space there is for creativity, dialogue, or dissent. The organization becomes obedient but lifeless.

Control promises security but breeds silence. People stop experimenting. They wait for permission. They avoid risk. And the leader, mistaking compliance for commitment, believes everything is fine until innovation dries up and morale collapses.

The illusion of control convinces leaders they are protecting quality, but in truth, they are protecting comfort. Leadership is not about controlling outcomes; it is about cultivating environments where others can thrive.

True power comes not from command but from trust.

Ego also feeds on dependency. When leaders become the central problem-solvers, every challenge flows through them. It feels flattering, a sign of importance, but it breeds exhaustion for the leader and dependency for the team.

No one takes risks. Everyone looks up instead of around.

This is how faceless leadership becomes *faceless followership*. The team loses confidence in its own capacity, and the leader loses touch with the collective intelligence around them. Empowered teams do not need permission; they need purpose. When leadership becomes the bottleneck, ego has replaced empathy.

The most empowering sentence a leader can say is, *"You decide. I trust your judgment."*

In many organizations, busyness masquerades as progress. Leaders move from meeting to meeting, email to email, project to project, mistaking motion for meaning. The calendar is full, but the heart is empty. They check boxes faster but see people less. Faceless leadership thrives in this illusion because busyness feels noble. It signals commitment, sacrifice, and dedication, the very traits leaders are praised for.

But constant motion numbs awareness. Leaders lose time to think, listen, and reflect. They begin reacting instead of responding, performing instead of perceiving. Soon, they mistake noise for necessity, and urgency becomes culture. "When everything is urgent, nothing is important."

The illusion of progress feeds the ego but starves connection. It creates the appearance of momentum while eroding meaning. Leaders begin asking, *"How do we go faster?"* when they should be asking, *"Where are we actually going?"*

The illusion of progress often manifests as a culture of performance where image outweighs authenticity. Meetings become presentations. Emails become press releases. Feedback becomes filtered through fear of perception. People stop saying what is true because they are too busy saying what is acceptable.

In this kind of culture, leaders may seem accessible, but the connection is transactional. Relationships become conditional on usefulness rather than humanity. Faceless leadership thrives in such environments because everything looks impressive from the outside. Awards, recognition, and polished social media posts reinforce the image of success. But behind the surface, exhaustion simmers. The organization grows tired of pretending.

When performance replaces purpose, burnout becomes inevitable. "The danger of performing leadership is that it wins applause but loses alignment."

One of the cruelest paradoxes of faceless leadership is that it isolates the leader themselves. Surrounded by people but starved of honesty, the leader becomes a figurehead, respected, admired, but emotionally alone. Their position creates distance. People hesitate to challenge, comfort, or connect with them. Over time, leaders mistake isolation for independence. They start believing they do not need feedback, vulnerability, or support.

But even leaders need belonging. The healthiest leaders find spaces where they can take off the mask with mentors, peers, coaches, or communities that remind them they are human first and leader second. Without that grounding, leadership becomes self-referential, a feedback loop of assumptions and appearances. The leader becomes both the actor and the audience of their own performance.

Ego and illusion combine to create one of the deadliest forms of faceless leadership: certainty. Certainty kills curiosity, and curiosity is the root of growth. When leaders stop asking questions, they stop evolving. When they stop growing, the organization stagnates, even if it still looks busy.

A leader once confessed, "I used to think my team respected me because I had answers. Now I realize they trust me because I ask better questions."

Learning leaders are visible leaders. They model humility and remind everyone that mastery does not mean knowing everything, it means being open to anything. The moment a leader says, "I already know," their leadership stops breathing.

The Emotional Wake of Faceless Leadership

Faceless leadership leaves traces long after it is gone. You can feel it in teams that are polite but guarded, efficient but uninspired. You can see it in organizations that celebrate milestones but mourn meaning. These cultures recover slowly because they have forgotten what authentic leadership feels like.

To restore connection, a new kind of courage is required, not the courage to direct, but the courage to *reconnect*. Leaders must be willing to unlearn the habits that made them successful but disconnected. That unlearning is not weakness; it is evolution. "The most courageous act of leadership is not standing tall but stepping closer."

Faceless leadership does not begin with failure; it begins with fatigue. Leaders lose their humanity one small compromise at a time: one ignored feeling, one unspoken truth, one moment of pretending to know when they do not. To name these moments is not to assign blame but to invite awareness. Because what remains unconscious will always lead unconsciously.

Below are *five common pitfalls of faceless leadership,* the quiet ways good intentions erode into disconnection, and how to find the way back.

1. Image Over Integrity

When leaders prioritize looking right over being real, integrity becomes conditional. They craft messages rather than meaning, and people begin to follow optics rather than truth. Integrity is not just moral; it is relational. It is the alignment between what we say, what we do, and how others experience us. When those three things align, trust grows. When they do not, even small inconsistencies become cultural cracks.

The antidote to this pitfall is *authentic transparency*, telling the truth even when it feels risky. "Authenticity builds trust faster than perfection ever will." Real leaders do not protect their image; they protect integrity. Because the image fades when reality fails to match it.

2. Power Without Empathy

Power without empathy turns authority into intimidation. When leaders forget what it feels like to be led, they lose their ability to lead well. Empathy is not softness; it is situational awareness. It allows leaders to sense what logic cannot measure. The strongest leaders do not dominate rooms; they read them.

They listen before deciding, ask before acting, and understand before enforcing. Power with empathy creates courage; power without empathy creates compliance. And compliance, while convenient, is the enemy of commitment.

The antidote to this pitfall is *perspective taking,* deliberately seeking the view from another seat before deciding from your own. When leaders make empathy habitual, they build loyalty that lasts beyond policy.

3. Control Over Connection

Control promises certainty. Connection requires vulnerability. Most leaders choose control because it feels safer, but control limits growth. When leaders overdirect, they unintentionally teach people that their contribution is not trusted.

Soon, creativity collapses into compliance. Teams wait for orders rather than taking ownership. Connection does not require giving up authority; it requires giving up superiority.

The antidote to this pitfall is *shared ownership,* letting people shape the process, not just execute it. When leaders move from control to connection, they trade compliance for commitment and find that influence grows stronger when shared.

4. Busyness Over Presence

Busyness is the socially accepted addiction of leadership. It looks admirable, but it erases intimacy. When leaders are constantly rushing, they communicate, often unintentionally, that people are interruptions, not priorities.

Presence is not about time; it is about attention. It is the ability to be fully engaged in one conversation, one decision, one person at a time. A leader's presence is the organization's permission to pause.

When leaders slow down, others exhale. "Presence is leadership's most powerful productivity tool." The antidote to this pitfall is *intentional pause,* creating moments of stillness in meetings, one-on-ones, and decision cycles. When leaders stop moving for a moment, everyone starts meaning again.

5. Progress Without People

Progress is essential, but progress without people is vanity. Leaders obsessed with performance often mistake metrics for meaning. They measure outcomes but forget impact. They celebrate milestones but overlook morale.

True progress includes people in the process. The antidote to this pitfall is *participation,* inviting the team into the "why" and "how," not just the "what." When people co-author change, they invest emotionally in it.

That is when progress becomes partnership, not something done to people, but something built with them. "If people don't see themselves in the future, they'll resist it." Progress without people produces compliance; progress with people produces culture.

Reclaiming the Human Face of Leadership

The antidote to faceless leadership is not charisma; it is courage. The courage to be seen, to feel, to listen, and to admit imperfection.

When leaders choose to reconnect with humanity, both their own and others', everything changes. Meetings gain warmth. Conversations regain honesty. Results regain purpose.

It starts small:

A pause before speaking.

A question asked with genuine curiosity.

A decision made with empathy, not ego.

These gestures restore visibility, not in the literal sense, but in the emotional one. Visibility is not about being seen; it is about *seeing others*. "Leadership becomes faceless when it stops seeing faces."

To lead with face is to lead with grace, the grace to acknowledge imperfection, to practice humility, and to prioritize people over performance. When leaders do this, their presence becomes more than authority; it becomes a source of belonging.

Leadership Reflection Prompts

1. Where might I be protecting my image instead of living my integrity?

2. In what moments do I choose control over connection, and why?

3. When was the last time I slowed down long enough to truly listen?

4. How does my leadership make people feel, safe, seen, or small?

5. What one act of vulnerability could make me a more present leader this week?

The antidote to faceless leadership is not more visibility; it is more vulnerability. Faithful leadership is the quiet courage to keep showing up as human, even when it feels safer to hide behind strategy, structure, or screens. To lead with face is to lead with empathy, clarity, and courage.

People follow not titles or talent, but truth. Because when leadership has a face, it gives everyone else permission to have one too. And that, more than any plan or performance metric, is what makes leadership timeless.

7

PUTTING A FACE ON THE VISION

The organization had a beautiful vision statement. It was bold, inspiring, and perfectly worded, every phrase polished by committees, consultants, and communication experts. It looked flawless on paper.

But when the leader stood before her team and read it aloud, the room stayed quiet. People nodded respectfully, but their faces did not change. There was no spark, no recognition, no shared energy.

When she finished, someone asked gently, "What does that mean for us?" The question stunned her. She had assumed her passion, belief, and commitment were enough to carry the message. In that moment, she realized the vision had no face. It had direction but no emotion, purpose but no people, words but no story. It was an elegant sentence that no one could see themselves in.

Over the next few months, she began asking questions instead of giving speeches.

"What would this vision look like in your world?"

"How would this change your day to day?"

"What part of this do you want to be part of?"

The answers surprised her. The same words that had once felt abstract began to take shape through people's experiences: teachers describing their classrooms, staff envisioning new ways to connect with clients, volunteers seeing hope in the faces they served. The vision finally had a heartbeat, not because it changed, but because it became visible.

A vision becomes powerful the moment people can see themselves inside it. Every organization has a vision; few have one that people can feel. That gap between statement and story, between aspiration and embodiment, is where most leadership efforts stumble.

A vision that lives only on slides, websites, or walls is an artifact, not a force. A true vision does not live in language; it lives in people. It must be seen, spoken, and shared in ways that make it personal. When people can picture how their work contributes to something larger than themselves, they move from compliance to conviction.

But when vision remains abstract, full of lofty phrases like "excellence," "innovation," and "impact," people cannot see themselves in it. They may admire it, but they cannot connect to it. The problem is not ambition; it is a lack of *human translation.*

Leaders often see the future clearly but forget that others must feel it emotionally before they can commit to it intellectually. A living vision breathes. It has rhythm, texture, and emotion. It evolves as people engage with it, interpret it, and embody it. Unlike a static mission statement, a living vision is relational. It invites participation. It is not declared; it is discovered.

There are three essential dimensions that make a vision come alive: Purpose, People, and Practice.

1. Purpose: The Why Behind the What

Purpose is the emotional anchor of a vision, the reason it matters beyond profit or prestige. It gives meaning to effort, sacrifice, and change. When a vision is grounded in purpose, it does not just tell people what to do; it reminds them *why it is worth doing.*

A teacher does not stay late grading papers because of test scores. A nurse does not arrive early for shift change because of protocol. They do it because they believe in the *impact* behind the action. Purpose connects the task to transformation.

When leaders articulate that connection clearly, consistently, and compassionately, people stop working for the organization and start working *through it*. They see their contribution as part of something sacred. Purpose is not a paragraph; it is the heartbeat behind every sentence.

2. People: The Heartbeat of the Vision

A vision without people is a picture without color. Leaders often fall in love with ideas, but ideas do not execute themselves. People bring ideas to life. They shape them through creativity, emotion, and shared ownership.

For a vision to have a face, people must see their reflection in it. This means inviting them into the conversation, not after the vision is complete, but while it is being crafted. It means asking, "What does this mean to you?" instead of telling them what it means to you.

When people co-author the vision, they protect it as if it were their own. When they are excluded, they treat it like someone else's agenda. The face of a vision is not the leader's; it is the collective reflection of everyone who believes in it.

3. Practice: Turning Vision into Behavior

Even the most inspiring vision fades without practice. Vision becomes visible when it shapes daily choices about how meetings are run, how conflicts are resolved, and how success is celebrated. Practice turns intention into integrity.

If the vision says "collaboration," but meetings reward hierarchy, the message breaks. If it says "innovation," but mistakes are punished, the message dies. An organization's daily rituals are its truest communication strategy.

Every decision, every norm, and every conversation either reinforces or contradicts the vision. Leaders who want to put a face on their vision must live it first, visibly and consistently, because nothing teaches faster than example.

A leader does not *own* the vision; they *embody* it. The leader's face becomes the first mirror through which people interpret the message. If the leader is guarded, the vision feels unsafe. If the leader is inspired, the vision feels possible. If the leader is consistent, the vision feels credible.

Leaders are not just communicators of vision; they are demonstrations of it. That is why authenticity matters more than articulation. People may not remember every word of a speech, but they never forget how a leader's conviction made them feel.

Vision is not taught; it is transferred through presence.
Faceless leadership turns vision into currency, a slogan to motivate performance rather than a story to inspire purpose. People become tools of productivity instead of carriers of meaning. The future becomes something to manage instead of something to co-create.

When this happens, even the most inspiring goals start to feel heavy. Without connection, vision becomes pressure instead of possibility. Leaders can sense this shift when energy changes, when teams start asking, "How much longer?" instead of "What's next?"

That is when it is time to pause, breathe, and rehumanize the message.

Ask again:

Who is this vision really for?

What will it look like in their world, not just mine?

What emotion do I want this vision to create when people hear it?

Because the real work of leadership is not *selling* a vision; it is *sharing* one.

When a vision has a face, it does something remarkable. It starts to attract people who align with its values and energy. It becomes a gravitational force. Recruitment becomes easier because the message resonates deeper than a job description. Retention improves because people feel they belong to something meaningful. Innovation expands because people feel trusted to shape the future.

The face of a living vision conveys belonging and an open invitation to be part of something bigger. When people see themselves in the story, they do not need motivation; they have meaning. And that is what gives a vision life.

The best visions are not sold; they are shared through stories that feel like mirrors.

Purpose provides a vision with gravity. It anchors ambition in meaning. Without purpose, vision drifts into slogans, temporary, replaceable, and emotionally shallow. With purpose, vision becomes a steady compass, guiding and deeply human.

Leaders often make the mistake of leading with "what" instead of "why." They describe projects, goals, and deliverables but forget to communicate the heart behind them. Purpose answers the question every follower is silently asking: *Why should I care?*

A vision that lacks purpose might inspire short-term enthusiasm, but it will not sustain long-term loyalty. People do not follow tasks; they follow transformation.

When leaders make purpose visible by tying daily work to enduring impact, they bridge the gap between personal values and organizational goals.

In education, the purpose is not just to raise test scores; it is to ignite curiosity and confidence in young minds. In healthcare, it is not only about treating illness but about restoring dignity. In community work, it is not about delivering programs but about creating belonging.

These deeper "whys" fuel resilience when the path gets hard.

Purpose is the invisible current that carries people through visible storms. Leaders who revisit purpose regularly keep their teams anchored in meaning, not just metrics.

Purpose gives clarity, but it also gives *calm*. When people understand *why* something matters, they can tolerate uncertainty about *how* it unfolds. Leaders often underestimate the emotional stability that purpose provides. In times of change, purpose reassures people that even if the process shifts, the values remain. This emotional continuity builds trust. When people know *why,* they can handle almost any *what.*

The best leaders repeat purpose constantly, not because people forget, but because they need reminding. Purpose must be visible in every meeting, decision, and message. Repetition does not create fatigue when the message carries meaning.

If purpose is the heartbeat, people are the face. No vision becomes reality until it passes through people's hands, hearts, and habits. Leaders who understand this do not just broadcast the vision; they *translate* it. They take big ideas and make them feel personal by telling stories, not just sharing strategies. They connect the future to real lives, not just charts and timelines.

A vision becomes believable when it is visible in human stories. For example:

⇒ When an educator describes how a new initiative helped a student find confidence.

⇒ When a manager shares how an employee's innovation saved the company time and resources.

⇒ When a community leader celebrates how collective action turned a neighborhood project into pride.

These moments make vision tangible. They give the abstract a face, and that is where momentum begins. A vision without story is direction without destination.

A vision gains strength through participation. Leaders can create this by asking, "How do *you* see yourself contributing to this?" That single question transforms followers into co-authors. People who help shape the vision do not just follow it; they defend it. Shared ownership does not dilute authority, it distributes energy. It aligns personal goals with collective purpose.

This is how communities, companies, and classrooms move from compliance to commitment: when everyone can point to the same direction and say, *"We built this together."* The face of the vision becomes plural, *not mine, but ours.*

Putting a face on the vision also means designing it with empathy. Empathy does not soften communication; it strengthens strategy. When leaders take time to understand how their vision affects different groups, they build emotional alignment before structural change.

Before launching a new initiative, empathetic leaders ask:

Who might feel left out or overwhelmed by this change?

What support will they need to thrive?

How can we make this transition feel like a partnership, not a punishment?

By anticipating emotions instead of just outcomes, leaders prevent resistance before it happens. Empathy ensures that the vision feels inclusive, that everyone can find themselves within it. The best visions are not designed *for* people; they are designed *with* them.

Vision is not a speech; it is a standard. It gains credibility not from how beautifully it is described, but from how consistently it is demonstrated. When leaders say one thing and do another, the message collapses. When they model the behavior they expect, the message multiplies.

Every choice a leader makes, what they praise, what they ignore, what they repeat, either reinforces or erodes the vision. That is why *practice* gives the vision its face. It shows up in how decisions are made, how people are treated, and how leaders respond when no one is watching. Vision without practice is performance. Vision with practice becomes culture.

People do not follow vision statements; they follow visible standards.

Measurement matters, but it cannot replace meaning. Metrics should *mirror* the vision, not distort it. For example, if the vision is about empowerment, measure growth in confidence, participation, and initiative, not just output. If the vision is about inclusion, track belonging, representation, and voice, not just demographics. Leaders must ensure that what gets measured still feels human. Otherwise, success becomes technically correct but emotionally hollow.

The goal is not just to meet the vision but to *manifest* it, making it visible at every layer of experience. The most powerful leaders do not communicate vision once; they *embody* it every day.

Consistency is what transforms vision into identity. It tells people, "This is who we are, not just what we do." When people see that alignment, trust becomes instinctive. They stop questioning intent because they can see integrity. This does not mean perfection; it means predictability. People trust leaders who stay steady in purpose, even when outcomes fluctuate.

Consistency does not mean doing everything right; it means doing the right things regularly. A consistent leader gives people emotional safety in seasons of change. That safety allows the vision to grow because people take more risks when they trust the ground beneath them.

When leaders live the vision visibly, others begin to emulate it naturally. Culture is simply *vision in repetition*. Every time someone acts in alignment with the vision, they reinforce its presence. Every story told, every success celebrated, every failure reframed builds a collective memory of what the organization stands for.

The leader may spark the vision, but culture sustains it. When that happens, the vision no longer belongs to one person or one department; it belongs to everyone. It becomes a living force that defines the present as much as it describes the future.

When vision is abstract, it inspires admiration but not action. When vision has a face, it becomes something people can live, not just follow. Across cultures, industries, and communities, the visions that endure share four universal qualities, four "faces" that make them tangible, relatable, and resilient.

The Four Faces of a Living Vision

1. **Clarity** – It must be understood.

2. **Credibility** – It must be believed.

3. **Connection** – It must be felt.

4. **Consistency** – It must be lived.

Together, these faces turn aspiration into alignment and alignment into action.

1. Clarity: Making the Vision Understandable

Clarity is kindness. It removes confusion so energy can flow toward purpose. Leaders often underestimate how much interpretation their words require. What is clear to them can be cloudy to others, not because people are not listening, but because they process through different experiences, fears, and priorities.

A clear vision paints the picture in color, not grayscale. It answers questions before they arise:

What are we moving toward?

Why does it matter?

What will success look and feel like for us?

Clarity requires simplicity without dilution, expressed in human language. When leaders choose clarity over complexity, they invite participation. People cannot contribute to what they do not comprehend.

Clarity is not dumbing down; it is lifting everyone to the same horizon. The clearer the vision, the easier it becomes for others to see their place within it.

2. Credibility: Making the Vision Believable

A vision is only as strong as the trust behind it. When leaders speak of transformation but act with hesitation, credibility erodes. When they promise change but preserve comfort, people disengage.

Credibility grows through alignment between message and model. If a leader wants innovation, they must reward experimentation. If they wish to build trust, they must show transparency. If they want collaboration, they must practice humility.

Credibility does not demand perfection; it requires integrity. People forgive mistakes faster than inconsistency. They can accept setbacks as long as the leader stays honest about them.

A believable vision is one carried by believable people. When leaders embody the message, the organization no longer needs slogans. The leader becomes the proof.

3. Connection: Making the Vision Felt

Connection turns vision into emotion. It is the difference between knowing the direction and *feeling* the destination. When a vision connects, people see themselves as part of something larger than their own job description. It awakens belonging.

Leaders create connection by using empathy as a communication tool. They translate abstract outcomes into stories of real human impact. Connection also requires listening, not just to respond, but to understand how the vision resonates or misses the mark.

A connected vision adapts; it grows through dialogue with those it touches. When people feel seen, they invest. When they feel invisible, they withdraw. That is why connected leaders speak *with* people, not at them.

A vision that does not move hearts will not move habits. Connection gives the vision its emotional face, one that smiles, listens, and responds.

4. Consistency: Making the Vision Sustainable

Consistency keeps the vision alive long after excitement fades. It transforms momentum into movement. Inconsistent leadership breeds confusion; people do not know which version of the vision to trust. Consistent leadership, on the other hand, builds safety. People know what to expect, and predictability breeds peace.

Consistency means showing up the same way in meetings, messages, and moments of crisis. It means that leadership's tone, behavior, and decisions reflect the same core values over time. It also means holding others accountable to those same standards, not through punishment, but through partnership.

When the leader is consistent, the culture becomes coherent. Coherent cultures create confident people.

Consistency is the quietest form of credibility. It is how vision becomes memory, how people internalize what leadership stands for without needing constant reminders.

The Four Faces in Action

Face of Vision	Core Question	Leadership Practice
Clarity	Do people understand what are we building?	Communicate the "why" simply and repeatedly.
Credibility	Do people believe we can achieve it?	Align behavior with message; model integrity.
Connection	Do people feel emotionally invested?	Translate goals into stories that show impact.

Face of Vision	Core Question	Leadership Practice
Consistency	Do people trust our follow through?	Reinforce values through steady actions.

A vision that embodies these four faces becomes *visible* not as a poster on the wall, but as a pattern in the organization's behavior. Every meeting, policy, and story reflects the shared future being built together. When a leader puts a face on the vision, it no longer belongs to them; it belongs to the community. The energy shifts from compliance to contribution. People stop waiting for direction and start creating it. They stop asking, "What do they want from us?" and start saying, "Here is what we are becoming."

This is what mature leadership looks like. It is when others carry the vision without constant prompting. In the end, the goal is not for people to remember the leader's face, but for them to remember the vision's meaning. A great leader does not make followers; they make the vision visible enough for everyone to lead.

Reflection Prompts

1. When people hear our vision, do they *see* themselves in it?

2. What parts of our vision feel clear, and which still feel abstract?

3. How am I modeling credibility through my everyday actions?

4. What emotions do people associate with our vision when I speak about it?

5. Where can I be more consistent, not in words, but in visible habits?

Putting a face on the vision is not about creating followers; it is about creating *believers*. Believers see, feel, and embody the future in everything they do. When vision has a face, people recognize themselves in it: their hopes, fears, efforts, and worth.

That recognition transforms a message into a movement. It turns work into meaning and organizations into communities. In a world often distracted by speed and spectacle, leaders who choose visibility with vulnerability, who put a face on their vision, offer people the rarest gift of all: a future they can *believe in* because they can *see themselves inside it.*

The future is not built by those who see the path most clearly. It is built by those who make the path feel like home.

8

COMMUNICATION THAT CONNECTS

Inner-Self Awareness

A ristotle said, "Knowing yourself is the beginning of wisdom." **One** of the most important qualities of effective leadership is the ability to know both your best and worst self. Often, our greatest strengths can also become our greatest liabilities. This happens because we operate comfortably within our own habits and perceptions, rarely challenged to see beyond them.

The same traits that helped us climb the organizational ladder may later hinder our ability to thrive once we reach the top. During leadership development seminars and team-building workshops, I often share stories from my Navy career, stories of both success and failure. I rose quickly through the ranks, earning promotions and responsibilities early. Yet, after attending key leadership seminars, I realized that my style of command had left too many subordinates emotionally exhausted in my wake.

Facing uncomfortable truths about ourselves is painful, but it is also freeing. The saying, "You shall know the truth, and the truth shall set you free," applies deeply here. When leaders embrace honest self-reflection, they unlock the foundation for growth and transformation.

Inner-Self Awareness demands openness and honesty:

Be willing to take a hard look inward.

Do not let ego interfere with overdue self-evaluation.

Be ready to release old habits that no longer serve you.

Listen to feedback without emotional rebuttal.

Apply the simple principle: Stop, Drop, and Roll.

Stop overlooking what others already see.

Drop your defenses.

Roll into a new mindset.

Inner-Self Awareness is the clear understanding of your own values, thoughts, strengths, weaknesses, passions, and motivations, and how they shape your actions and reactions. It is about recognizing your authentic self and understanding how your inner world connects with the people you lead.

When cultivated, it results in:

Better Decision-Making: Your choices align with your true self.

Emotional Regulation: You gain control over your inner responses.

Personal Growth: Awareness of strengths and weaknesses fuels improvement.

Improved Relationships: Empathy and communication deepen.

Increased Happiness: A stronger sense of purpose enhances satisfaction and stability.

You can develop Inner-Self Awareness through:

Mindfulness and Meditation: Focus on the present moment without judgment.

Journaling: Reflect regularly on your emotions, choices, and experiences.

Asking "What" Questions: Replace "Why am I like this?" with "What is happening?" to shift from blame to awareness.

Seeking Guidance: Work with a mentor, coach, or counselor for structured reflection.

Two

Awareness of the Needs of Those Around You

Effective leadership requires not only inner reflection but also awareness of the needs of others. Leaders who invest time in understanding the values and motivations of their teams build trust and resilience.

This awareness involves emotional intelligence, active listening, and reading nonverbal cues. Understanding basic human needs such as safety, belonging, and esteem helps leaders interpret behavior with empathy rather than judgment.

As philosopher Terry Warner of the Arbinger Institute described, seeing others as objects to use or obstacles to overcome destroys connection. When leaders genuinely value others, they build collaboration instead of control.

Awareness of others' needs leads to:

Stronger collaboration

Greater accountability

Higher innovation and engagement

Increased productivity and cooperation

Leaders can cultivate empathy and active listening through:

Putting themselves in others' positions.

Maintaining eye contact and eliminating distractions.

Listening to understand, not to respond.

Paying attention to tone and body language, which often reveal more than words.

Ask questions that invite openness:

"What are you hoping for?"

"What feels most important to you right now?"

"What support do you need to succeed?"

Recognize the difference between **needs** and **wants**. Needs are essential to well-being, while wants are preferences. Understanding this distinction helps leaders prioritize people's real concerns.

To apply this awareness in practice:

Recognize accomplishments. Celebrate progress and acknowledge effort.

Provide support. Address challenges with empathy, not correction.

Build trust. Make people feel valued, not used.

Leaders who do this consistently create environments where people feel safe to contribute and innovate.

Three

Awareness of the Power of Silence

Silence is a powerful leadership tool. It reduces noise, external and internal, and makes space for clarity, creativity, and connection.

Intentional silence strengthens emotional health, focus, and self-awareness. It encourages reflection and opens the door to wisdom and spiritual growth. Silence is not emptiness; it is active awareness.

Benefits of Silence:

Mental Health: Reduces stress, anxiety, and tension.

Focus and Clarity: Clears mental clutter and sharpens perception.

Self-Awareness: Creates space to observe thoughts and emotions.

Spiritual and Creative Growth: Connects the inner self with deeper insight.

Communication: Creates space for listening and conveys understanding.

Silence works by creating **internal space**, a mental clearing where insight can form. It also activates the brain's **default mode network**, which enhances problem-solving and creativity.

Different faith traditions use silence as a spiritual practice:

Hinduism: The discipline of *Mauna* (voluntary silence) cultivates higher consciousness.

Judaism: Silence symbolizes wisdom and spiritual depth.

Islam: Teachings encourage speaking only with virtue or remaining silent.

Silence teaches leaders patience and presence. It invites others to speak and makes room for understanding.

Four

Awareness of One's Shadow Needs and Avoid Acting Them Out Inappropriately

As mentioned in Chapter One, Carl Jung offers profound insight into the concept of the *shadow self*. Exploring this hidden side of our nature is essential for achieving emotional balance, wholeness, and authentic leadership. The shadow represents the parts of ourselves that remain unconscious: traits, impulses, and desires we deny or suppress. Although invisible, the shadow is always active and often emerges in unexpected ways.

For leaders, acknowledging the shadow is critical. Leadership carries weight: responsibility, visibility, and the pressure of others' expectations. Understanding your shadow helps you recognize the unseen motives and insecurities that influence behavior. This awareness deepens authenticity, emotional intelligence, and empathy. It also helps prevent the projection of personal struggles onto others.

Benefits of Engaging Your Shadow

Increased self-awareness (of motivations, strengths, and weaknesses)

Improved emotional intelligence (greater ability to understand and manage emotions)

Enhanced authenticity (the freedom to be genuine and transparent)

Greater self-confidence (accepting imperfections without shame)

Emotional healing (integrating past wounds into wisdom)

Stronger relationships (more empathy and honesty in interactions)

Reduced conflict (less projection of personal negativity)

Heightened creativity (releasing suppressed potential)

Continuous personal growth (learning from discomfort)

Greater resilience (building capacity to face challenges with calm)

The Consequences of Ignoring the Shadow

When leaders refuse to confront their shadow traits such as selfishness, jealousy, or arrogance, they unconsciously project them onto others. This process, known as projection, distorts perception and damages trust. On a larger scale, unacknowledged collective shadows can create cultures of blame, cruelty, and systemic conflict.

Practical Ways to Begin Shadow Work

Notice your triggers. Pay attention to people or behaviors that evoke strong emotions in you. They often mirror something unresolved within yourself.

Observe your feelings. Instead of judging them, ask what message they carry.

Record your dreams. Nighttime imagery can reveal unconscious conflicts or desires.

Jung warned that collective progress depends on individual responsibility. Leaders who face their own shadows create healthier organizational cultures. When a leader models honest self-examination, others follow.

Be gentle but truthful with yourself. Self-awareness is not self-criticism; it is self-liberation.

Five

Awareness Not to Take Yourself Too Seriously

When I was promoted to Lieutenant Commander in the U.S. Navy, a close friend called and asked, "When you get to your new duty station, are you going to expect your troops to work as hard as you?" Without hesitation, I said, "Absolutely." His reply changed my perspective: "Then you will fail."

He knew me well. He knew I was driven, the first to arrive, the last to leave, the one who pushed hardest for results. But his words made me realize that the same intensity that fueled my success could also limit my leadership. My strength had become my liability.

Taking yourself too seriously often comes from perfectionism, fear of judgment, and overattachment to control. It manifests in overthinking, defensiveness, and an inability to relax.

Signs You Are Taking Yourself Too Seriously

Constant anxiety or pressure to perform

Black-and-white thinking (everything is either success or failure)

Unrealistic expectations of yourself or others

Avoidance of risk or new experiences

Defensiveness and overreaction to feedback

Obsession with perfection and image

Ways to Lighten Up

Use humor. Laugh at your mistakes and allow imperfection to be part of growth.

Separate thoughts from facts. Not every worry reflects truth.

Stay grounded. When overthinking, reconnect to your senses by noticing the sound of your environment, the feel of your chair, or the taste of your coffee.

Label unhelpful thoughts. Give them names like "the I am not good enough story." This defuses their power.

Release past mistakes. Learn from them but do not live in them.

Focus on relationships. Prioritize connection over performance.

Leadership demands perspective. The moment you stop laughing at yourself, you risk losing touch with others.

These five forms of awareness: of self, others, silence, shadow, and balance, are seeds of sustainable leadership. They grow through humility, patience, and daily practice. If something feels unnatural at first, pause and try again later. Leadership growth is not about perfection; it is about persistence and presence.

Be strong enough to lead and humble enough to be led. Sometimes the people you guide will help you see the limits you cannot see in yourself.

In my close I would like to share one of my personal Daily Bread Devotionals that I think get the very heart of what I have attempted to do through these two chapters regarding…working together and generating group synergy.

Enjoy and be blessed!

Reflection: *It Takes Two*

Climbing Jamaica's Dunn's River Falls is both thrilling and challenging. Water rushes over smooth rocks as climbers make their way upward. For a teenager named JW, who was sight-impaired with only a pinhole of vision, it seemed nearly impossible.

But JW was determined to climb, and his friend Josiah was determined to help him. Josiah became JW's eyes, guiding his hands and feet. JW became Josiah's heart, showing him, what courage looks like.

Life is much the same. We are not meant to climb alone. King Solomon wrote, "Two people are better than one, for they can help each other succeed" (Ecclesiastes 4:9). Together, JW and Josiah reached the top. Neither fell, and neither failed.

True leadership reflects this same truth: the work is best done together. Success is not achieved through independence but through interdependence. Each person brings a gift the other lacks, and together they reach higher ground.

At 8:00 a.m., the leader sent a well-written, detailed email announcing a new organizational restructuring. Every line was precise and logical. By 9:00 a.m., her inbox was full, not of complaints but of confusion.

Her team was not angry; they were unsure how to feel. Some asked polite questions, others said nothing, though rumors began circulating. She reread her message and realized nothing was factually wrong, but something was missing. She had written from her head, not her heart.

Information does not equal communication. Communication begins when meaning meets emotion.

That morning, she learned one of the most important lessons in leadership: *clarity without connection creates confusion*. It is not enough to be correct; leaders must also be *compassionate*. Leadership communication is never neutral. Every word, tone, and pause either builds connection or creates distance. You can say all the right things, but if people do not feel seen or respected in how you say them, the message will not land. Communication is not just a skill; it is a reflection of leadership character. How a leader communicates in moments of uncertainty reveals who they truly are.

When tension rises, do they react or respond?

When feedback comes, do they defend or listen?

When mistakes happen, do they shame or teach?

These are not just communication choices; they are *culture-shaping behaviors*. The way leaders communicate becomes the model for how everyone else interacts. If a leader speaks with empathy, teams mirror empathy. If a leader communicates with fear, teams learn to hide.

Words create atmosphere. Atmosphere creates trust. And trust, more than talent, determines whether a message transforms or merely transmits.

Connection in communication does not happen by accident. It happens by alignment. It occurs when four elements work together:

1. **Trust:** People believe the speaker's intent is genuine.

2. **Tone:** The emotional delivery matches the message's purpose.

3. **Timing:** The message arrives when people are ready to hear it.

4. **Transparency:** The truth is shared clearly and respectfully.

Let us look at each briefly.

1. Trust: The Foundation of Listening

People do not listen deeply to leaders they do not trust. Trust makes listeners emotionally and mentally available to receive information. It is built not through grand speeches, but through small consistencies. When people see that a leader's words align with actions, they stop doubting intent and start engaging meaningfully.

Leaders who want to strengthen connections should ask:
"Do people believe I mean what I say and say what I mean?"
If not, the issue is not communication skill but relational credibility.

2. Tone: The Emotion Behind the Message

Tone is the bridge between words and feelings. A leader can deliver the same sentence in two ways and create opposite results. "I need this by Friday." Said with urgency, it motivates. Said with impatience, it intimidates. Tone carries what text cannot: empathy, respect, humility, or arrogance.

In the digital age, tone is even more critical because messages often travel without body language or facial cues. That is why emotionally intelligent leaders *emphasize humanity.* They add context, warmth, and gratitude where text might otherwise sound cold. Tone does not just affect understanding; it defines trustworthiness.

3. Timing: The Rhythm of Readiness

Even the best message fails when delivered at the wrong moment. A great communicator knows when to speak and when to wait. They sense when people are emotionally ready to absorb truth. Timing requires empathy, not strategy. It is about feeling the room, noticing the mood, and respecting capacity.

Delivering constructive feedback when someone is already overwhelmed may make them feel criticized rather than supported. Waiting until they can listen openly transforms the same input into growth. Good leaders schedule communication. Great leaders *sense* it. Connection happens in rhythm, not in rush.

4. Transparency: The Currency of Trust

People can handle bad news. They cannot handle *being surprised* by it. Transparency does not mean sharing everything; it means sharing what matters with honesty and humility. When leaders withhold information out of fear, they create confusion and suspicion. When they overexplain with empathy, they build confidence.

Transparency tells people: "You are capable of hearing the truth." That message alone strengthens belonging. Transparency requires courage because truth is vulnerable. Yet vulnerability in leadership is what makes communication real.

Leaders often assume communication is about control: managing narratives, protecting image, and preventing chaos. But connection comes not from control, but from courage. When leaders speak openly and humanly, they create psychological safety, the invisible permission for others to speak truth in return. Without that safety, organizations suffer from what can be called truth decay:

Employees stop telling leaders what they need to hear.

Teams avoid conflict but increase resentment.

Innovation fades because fear fills the silence.

Connected communication reverses that cycle. It turns silence into conversation and conversation into progress. When people feel safe to speak, honesty replaces politics, curiosity replaces fear, and collaboration replaces compliance. Culture changes not through slogans but through conversations that feel safe enough to be real.

Communication is not what you say; it is what others feel safe enough to say back.

There are two kinds of leadership communication: *transactional* and *transformational.*

Transactional communication delivers information. It is efficient but shallow, focusing on the "what" and "when." It keeps systems running but rarely changes hearts.

Transformational communication builds relationship. It engages emotion, curiosity, and meaning, focusing on the "why" and "how." It connects purpose to people.

Both are necessary, but only one sustains trust. Great leaders move between both, using transactional clarity while maintaining transformational connection. Every message is an opportunity to strengthen belonging or reinforce distance. Every conversation either feeds culture or fractures it.

Listening is not a pause between talking; it is the practice of presence. It is how leaders discover what is not being said, where tension lives, and where hope still exists. Listening well is leadership's quiet superpower. When people feel heard, they begin to heal. And when they heal, they begin to trust again.

Listening creates visibility. It reminds people that their voice matters and their story counts.

Leadership begins not with a statement, but with a question: "Tell me what this means to you."

Empathy is the foundation of all meaningful communication. It allows leaders to translate information into understanding and direction into trust.

Empathy does not mean agreeing with everything someone says; it means caring enough to understand *why* they are saying it. Leaders who communicate with empathy speak *to* people, not *at* them. They listen to learn, not to label.

Empathy begins with awareness, pausing long enough to say, "I see that this matters to you." That single acknowledgment does more to connect people than a dozen solutions.

Empathy is not the act of fixing pain; it is the art of witnessing it.

Most communication breakdowns do not happen because people fail to *hear*; they happen because people fail to *understand*. When leaders listen only for facts, they miss feelings. Yet feelings are what drive behavior.

A team member might say, "We are stretched too thin." A transactional leader replies, "We will add another meeting to review workload." An empathetic leader pauses and asks, "What is making the workload feel unsustainable?"

That question opens the door to ownership and trust. Empathy *turns* frustration into feedback, fear into insight, and silence into signal.

When people are upset, their words are often messy, defensive, or unclear. An empathetic communicator listens for what lies *beneath* the words: the need to feel heard, valued, or safe.

An emotionally intelligent leader asks, "What story is this emotion trying to tell?" This does not just calm conflict; it deepens connection. Empathy does not weaken authority; it strengthens credibility. People trust leaders who can hold both firmness and compassion at once.

While empathy connects the heart, clarity connects the mind. Without clarity, even the kindest communication can create confusion. Over time, confusion breeds frustration.

Clarity does not mean oversimplifying; it means removing ambiguity so people can focus on contribution, not interpretation.

Leaders who communicate with clarity:

Use plain language instead of jargon.

Define expectations instead of implying them.

Separate fact from opinion.

Summarize key points to confirm understanding.

Clarity creates momentum because it replaces uncertainty with alignment. Clarity is what turns empathy into execution.

Ambiguity creates emotional fatigue. When people are unsure what is expected, they spend energy guessing how to act, what to prioritize, and what success means. Uncertainty erodes trust faster than mistakes.

Clarity, on the other hand, creates safety. When people know where they stand, they take risks, ask questions, and innovate. The clearest communicators are often the most trusted because they reduce anxiety by giving people something solid to hold onto.

Clarity says, "You do not have to read between the lines. I will tell you what matters."

Speaking with Structure and Simplicity

The most effective leaders communicate complex ideas through *simple structures.* They might say:

1. Here is what we are doing.

2. Here is why it matters.

3. Here is what we need from you.

This structure works across settings, from boardrooms to classrooms, because it is predictable, transparent, and respectful of people's time.

Simplicity is not a lack of sophistication; it is a mark of mastery. When leaders simplify without condescending, they make others feel capable and confident. Confidence builds connection.

People do not remember what is complicated; they remember what is clear.

Connection does not mean comfort. The most meaningful communication often happens in uncomfortable moments, during feedback, conflict, or change. Courageous communication means saying what needs to be said with empathy and respect. It is the balance of honesty and humanity.

Most leaders avoid difficult conversations not because they lack skill, but because they fear emotional fallout such as disappointment, defensiveness, or disapproval. Yet silence does not protect relationships; it slowly poisons them. Avoided conversations become invisible resentments. When leaders speak truth early and kindly, they prevent disconnection later.

Honesty without empathy is cruelty. Empathy without honesty is avoidance. True connection requires both.

Courageous communicators reframe feedback as *investment,* not *interrogation.* They deliver it with the intent to help, not to humiliate. They focus on *behavior,* not *identity.* For example, instead of saying, "You are not reliable," they might say, "When reports are late, it affects the whole team. How can I support you in managing the workload?" That phrasing shifts the tone from accusation to collaboration. It makes feedback feel like partnership, not punishment.

Feedback that connects always begins with care. Every leader will face moments when truth feels heavy, when they must deliver bad news, address underperformance, or acknowledge failure. In those moments, tone matters more than terminology. People do not expect perfection; they expect presence. They want to know their leader sees them, not just the situation.

The most powerful words in leadership are not *directives*. They are *declarations of humanity:*

"I know this is hard."

"I do not have all the answers, but we will figure it out together."

"Your feelings make sense."

These phrases communicate care while maintaining clarity. They say, "We can face the truth, and we can do it with grace." It is easy to connect when the news is good. The true test of leadership communication is how connection survives discomfort. When leaders are willing to speak truth kindly, people feel respected even in disagreement. They may not like the message, but they will trust the messenger.

People trust leaders who do not hide truth behind comfort. Courage does not mean removing fear; it means speaking through it. When fear is met with empathy and clarity, it transforms into trust.

Empathy, clarity, and courage are not separate traits; they are a system.

Empathy connects hearts.

Clarity connects minds.

Courage connects truth.

When all three align, communication becomes transformational. It invites understanding without confusion, honesty without harm, and belonging without blindness. These three elements form the language of leadership that lasts. People may forget strategy, but they never forget how it felt to be understood, respected, and told the truth.

The future of leadership is not louder communication; it is deeper connection. Every message carries two layers: the content and the connection. Most leaders focus on what they say, but the lasting impact depends on how people feel when they hear it.

Connection-driven communication is not about talking more. It is about listening better, thinking clearer, and responding truer. The best leaders speak from a place of **Presence, Precision, Permission,**

and Purpose. These four elements form the architecture of connection, simple enough to remember and profound enough to transform.

1. Presence: Be Fully There

Presence is the quiet power of attention. It says, "I am with you right now, not just near you." When leaders are distracted, checking phones during meetings or half-listening while multitasking, people feel it instantly. Distraction communicates disinterest. But when a leader is fully present, they create safety. People relax, open up, and share what they really think.

Presence is not about time; it is about *attunement.* Even five minutes of focused attention builds more trust than an hour of divided focus. Presence makes people feel visible, and being seen is a fundamental human need.

Presence turns communication into connection and conversation into care.

Leadership Practice:

Put away distractions during one-on-one meetings.

Repeat back what you hear to confirm understanding.

Allow pauses. Silence often invites truth.

2. Precision: Say It So It Stays

Precision gives communication power and direction. It is not about perfectionism; it is about intentionality. In leadership, vague language creates vague results. Precision builds alignment because it turns vision into shared understanding.

Precision does not mean using big words; it means choosing *true* words. For example:

Instead of saying "ASAP," specify "by Friday at noon."

Instead of "we need to improve," define how and why.

Instead of "we will figure it out," outline the next small step.

Specificity creates accountability, and accountability builds trust. Precision is compassion in disguise because it spares people from guessing.

Leadership Practice:

Use clear frameworks when presenting ideas.

Define success in measurable, relatable terms.

Replace jargon with human language.

3. Permission: Invite Truth

Permission means creating a space where honesty feels safe, where people can speak freely without fear of consequence. In many organizations, people remain silent not because they lack ideas, but because they lack permission. They fear judgment, dismissal, or retaliation.

Leaders who grant permission turn communication into collaboration. They do not just *allow* feedback; they *welcome* it. They ask questions such as:

"What am I missing?"

"What is one thing you would do differently?"

"I might be wrong here. What do you think?"

These questions flatten hierarchy and elevate humanity. They remind people that leadership is a role, not a rank. Permission is the soil where truth can grow.

Leadership Practice:

Open meetings with a question, not a directive.

Thank people for honesty, even when it is hard to hear.

Reward candor with gratitude, not defensiveness.

4. Purpose: Speak from Values, Not Ego

Purpose gives communication meaning. It keeps words aligned with integrity and values. When communication lack's purpose, it becomes reactive and shaped by emotion instead of intention. But when leaders pause to reconnect with their "why," their words gain resonance.

Purpose transforms statements into stories and instructions into inspiration. It ensures that what we say not only informs minds but also moves hearts. Purpose is what makes words worth remembering.

Purpose-driven communication always asks:

Does this message reflect our values?

Does it serve people, or just protect image?

Does it move us closer to connection or farther from it?

Leadership Practice:

Anchor every communication in "why it matters."

Use purpose statements to guide difficult conversations.

Align tone with intent: calm when others are anxious, clear when others are confused.

The Framework in Action

Element	What It Means	What It Builds	Leadership Practice
Presence	Full attention and Attunement	Trust and Safety	Listen fully; minimize Distractions
Precision	Clear, specific, intentional language	Alignment and Accountability	Define success clearly; Remove Ambiguity
Permission	Psychological safety for truth telling	Honesty and Innovation	Invite dissent; reward vulnerability

Element	What It Means	What It Builds	Leadership Practice
Purpose	Values based and meaning driven communication	Credibility and Belonging	Anchor messages in shared "why"

When these four elements work together, communication becomes culture. People stop guarding their words and start sharing their wisdom. Dialogue replaces debate. Curiosity replaces control. Trust replaces fear.

That is when communication stops being a tool and becomes a *bridge.* Every message a leader sends echoes through the organization. The tone of leadership becomes the tone of culture. If leaders speak with empathy, clarity, and consistency, their teams learn to do the same. If they lead through fear, confusion, or avoidance, that becomes the language of the system.

Culture does not only reflect what leaders *believe;* it reflects how they *speak.* Every culture speaks in the voice of its leaders. When leaders communicate with connection, they teach everyone else how to do the same. That is how empathy scales. That is how trust compounds. And that is how organizations begin to heal, one honest, human conversation at a time.

Reflection Prompts

1. When I speak, do people feel informed or included?

2. What distractions keep me from being fully present in communication?

3. When was the last time I invited truth, I was not ready to hear?

4. How does my communication reflect my values under pressure?

5. Which element: Presence, Precision, Permission, or Purpose. Do I need to strengthen most this month?

The greatest leaders are not remembered for what they said but for how they made people feel *heard.* Communication that connects is not about charisma or vocabulary. It is about *presence* that makes people feel safe, *precision* that builds confidence, *permission* that invites honesty, and *purpose* that inspires belief.

When those four qualities align, language becomes leadership. Words no longer inform; they *transform.* Because when communication carries empathy, clarity, and courage, it does more than transfer information, it transfers *trust*. And trust, more than talent or technology, sustains every vision worth building.

Leadership begins the moment words become bridges instead of walls.

9

MEETING RESISTANCE EYE TO EYE

The meeting was supposed to be energizing. The leader stood at the front of the room, introducing a new initiative designed to streamline processes, modernize technology, and bring everyone into the future. Her slides were sharp, her reasoning clear, and her excitement genuine.

But as she looked around, she sensed something she could not name. People were listening but not leaning in. A few nodded politely; others stared at their laptops or took notes without expression. The air felt thick, not hostile but hesitant.

She finished with optimism: "I know this change might feel big, but I believe in this team." Polite applause. No questions. That was the first sign of trouble.

Over the next few weeks, the same silence showed up in subtle ways: delayed responses to emails, missed deadlines, forgotten follow-ups. No one said they disagreed. No one openly resisted. But the work stalled.

In her frustration, she thought, *why will they not just get on board?* Then it clicked. *They were not resisting the idea; they were resisting the uncertainty behind it.* They were not defiant. They were afraid. Afraid of failure, of irrelevance, of change that might erase what they had worked so hard to build.

That was when she learned a truth every leader must face: resistance is not rejection, it is protection. People resist not because they do not care, but because something they care about feels at risk. The leader did not need to fight the resistance; she needed to understand it.

Resistance has a bad reputation. We label it as stubbornness, negativity, or lack of commitment. But most resistance is not rebellion; it is relationship. Resistance is communication. It is the emotional language people use when they do not yet have the words to express fear, doubt, or loss.

When leaders interpret resistance as opposition, they respond with persuasion: more data, more logic, more pressure. But persuasion rarely works on emotion. Connection does. People do not resist facts; they resist feeling unheard, unseen, or unsafe.

If a leader responds to resistance with frustration, the wall gets higher. But if they respond with curiosity, the wall becomes a window. Resistance is not the enemy of change; it is evidence that people still care.

Every act of resistance carries a hidden story.

⇒ A teacher reluctant to try a new curriculum is not lazy; she is protecting her students from confusion.

⇒ An employee pushing back against new software is not stubborn; he is anxious about losing confidence or competence.

⇒ A community group skeptical of new leadership is not negative; they are guarding trust that took years to build.

Resistance is often the body's natural response to emotional uncertainty. It is how people assert control when change feels imposed. The more leaders try to crush resistance, the more it multiplies. Suppression does not create commitment; it creates compliance. And compliance is fragile.

Leaders who want true transformation must learn to meet resistance *eye to eye,* not to eliminate it but to engage it.

When resistance meets empathy, it becomes revelation. It shows leaders where fear lives, where communication has failed, and where healing is needed.

Not all resistance is loud. Most of it whispers. It hides in behaviors such as:

⇒ Silence in meetings

⇒ Repeated "I'm fine" responses

⇒ Passive agreement followed by quiet withdrawal

⇒ Over analysis or perfectionism that delays action

These are not signs of laziness. They are signs of protection. They signal that people are managing emotional risk. The leader's job is to notice those cues early, before frustration turns into fracture.

Resistance becomes dangerous only when ignored. When leaders create space to discuss discomfort openly, saying, "I sense some hesitation; tell me what is behind it," they turn resistance into relationship. That single conversation can shift the energy in the room. When people feel seen, they no longer need to hide behind resistance.

Resistance is not an obstacle; it is a mirror reflecting where trust, communication, or clarity have broken down. It tells leaders what people are protecting: identity, pride, belonging, or past success. When leaders stop fighting resistance and start *listening* to it, they discover insight.

Resistance answers unasked questions:

⇒ Where do people feel excluded?

⇒ What values are being threatened?

⇒ What support have they not yet received?

A leader who sees resistance this way becomes both compassionate and strategic. Because resistance, when understood, becomes feedback. And feedback, when respected, becomes wisdom. Every act of resistance hides a truth leaders need to hear.

Even the most self-aware leaders can feel defensive when confronted with resistance. It can feel like rejection of their effort, vision, or leadership. That is why leaders must learn to separate *resistance to the idea* from *resistance to them as a person.* Often, the pushback is not personal; it is emotional. People are processing loss, not attacking leadership.

When leaders interpret resistance as disrespect, they move into control mode by lecturing, micromanaging, or withdrawing. That reaction only reinforces fear.

The antidote is humility. Leaders who can say, "I hear your hesitation; help me understand it," communicate strength through self-regulation. They model that resistance is not a threat but a teacher.

Every human being lives between two universal needs: the need for growth and the need for safety. Resistance is what happens when those two needs collide. Leaders love growth. Teams crave safety. The art of leadership is helping people feel *safe enough to grow*.

That is why emotional connection is not a soft skill. It is a strategic one. Without emotional safety, even the best vision feels threatening. With it, even the hardest change becomes possible. People do not fear change; they fear disconnection.

When leaders meet resistance eye to eye with empathy, honesty, and consistency, they transform fear into feedback and tension into trust.

Resistance exists on multiple levels. It is not only emotional; it is structural, relational, and sometimes deeply personal. When leaders see resistance only as a behavioral issue, they focus on surface symptoms instead of root causes. They respond with more communication, more incentives, or more pressure, but none of that addresses the *"why"* behind the *"what."*

To meet resistance eye to eye, leaders must learn to see it in three dimensions:

1. **Human Resistance**: emotional and psychological reactions.

2. **Systemic Resistance**: processes and norms that protect the status quo.

3. **Leadership Resistance**: the leader's own fear of vulnerability or loss of control.

Each dimension tells a different truth.

1. Human Resistance: The Language of Fear and Loss

Human resistance is the most visible and the most misunderstood. It shows up in the hesitation of teams, the tension in meetings, or the quiet that follows big announcements. At its core, human resistance is not about logic; it is about loss.

Change, even when positive, always asks people to give something up: familiarity, comfort, certainty, or identity. A teacher implementing a new system might lose the pride of mastery. An experienced employee might lose the comfort of predictability. A new hire might lose the illusion of control.

When people resist, they are not rejecting the future; they are grieving the past. Resistance is often grief wearing the mask of defiance.

The most effective leaders acknowledge that loss is real. They say, "I know this change impacts how you have always done things, and that is not easy." That simple sentence does something data cannot do. It validates emotion. And validation dissolves defensiveness.

Human resistance is rooted in biology. When faced with uncertainty, the brain perceives threat and activates the fight, flight, or freeze response. This is why people may respond to change with irritability, avoidance, or silence. Leaders who understand this do not take resistance personally. They regulate themselves first, then guide others back to calm through empathy and predictability.

Creating safety is not about avoiding discomfort. It is about reducing *uncertainty*. Predictable communication, consistent tone, and visible transparency help the nervous system relax enough to listen. The leader's calm becomes contagious.

When resistance shows up as anger or withdrawal, it is tempting to respond with logic. But logic alone cannot reach an emotional wound. Instead of debating, leaders can respond with curiosity:

⇒ "Tell me what feels hardest about this change."

⇒ "What part of this feels uncertain to you?"

⇒ "What would make this easier?"

These questions translate emotion into dialogue. When people feel emotionally seen, they move from defending to participating.

2. Systemic Resistance: When Structures Protect the Past

Even when individuals are ready to change, systems may not be. Systemic resistance occurs when organizational processes, policies, or unspoken norms make new behaviors difficult to sustain.

For example:

⇒ A school may say it values creativity but still reward conformity.

⇒ A company may claim to empower employees but punish mistakes.

⇒ A nonprofit may champion innovation but budget only for tradition.

In these cases, resistance is not personal; it is procedural. The system itself is protecting its comfort zone. Systems resist change in the same way people do, by defending what feels familiar.

Leaders often underestimate how much structure shapes behavior. Culture is not just emotion; it is repetition. What gets repeated becomes the real rule.

To identify systemic resistance, leaders can ask:

⇒ What behaviors are unintentionally rewarded here?

⇒ What stories do we tell ourselves about how things are done?

⇒ Where do our processes contradict our stated values?

Systemic resistance reveals itself in the gap between *intent and incentive*. If innovation is encouraged but failure is punished, resistance will always return.

Addressing systemic resistance requires redesign, not reprimand. Leaders must realign structures so that the new way is not only *possible* but *practical*.

Cultures do not shift because of slogans; they shift because of systems. If the system does not evolve, old habits reappear. The best leaders look beyond individual compliance and examine collective design. When systems reward curiosity, transparency, and collaboration, resistance fades. Not because fear disappears, but because growth feels supported.

Great leaders do not just motivate people to change; they modify the conditions that make change sustainable. Culture may eat strategy for breakfast, but systems feed culture every day.

Sustainable change happens when people no longer have to fight the system to do what is right. When procedures align with values, when communication reinforces purpose, and when accountability is practiced not just preached, culture begins to shift from performative to authentic. This is the moment when teams stop surviving inside an organization and start belonging to it.

Systems show people what is truly valued. If innovation is celebrated but punishment follows every mistake, the message is clear. If collaboration is encouraged but workloads reward isolation, the message is clear. Leaders must be intentional about aligning what they say with what their systems produce.

True cultural evolution requires leaders to examine every hidden mechanism policies, incentives, workflows, norms, traditions and ask a hard question: "Does this help us become who we say we are?" When the answer is yes, alignment strengthens. When the answer is no, the system becomes the roadmap for change.

Culture is not a motivational speech. It is the accumulation of daily behaviors shaped by the structures people work within. Change the structure, and you change the story.

Healthy systems create healthy people. Systems that center humanity well-being, fairness, dignity, clarity build trust that no speech can manufacture. When employees feel safe enough to speak the truth, confident enough to share ideas, and supported enough to take risks, culture shifts organically. Not from pressure, but from alignment.

Change becomes sustainable when leaders treat culture like an ecosystem rather than a slogan. Ecosystems thrive only when every part from the formal policies to the informal norms works in harmony.

Leaders must water what they want to grow, prune what threatens the mission, and remain vigilant about the conditions that surround their teams.

3. Leadership Resistance: When the Mirror Looks Back

The most difficult form of resistance to recognize is the leader's own. Leaders are human too. They fear failure, rejection, and loss of control just like everyone else. The difference is that their fear often hides behind authority.

Leadership resistance often shows up as overexplaining, micromanaging, or dismissing feedback. It appears in the instinct to protect image instead of exploring truth. The hardest resistance to face is our own.

Many leaders equate credibility with correctness. When challenged, they interpret it as disrespect instead of dialogue. But true credibility is not built on always being right; it is built on always being real.

When a leader says, "You might be right. Let's explore that," they model both confidence and humility. That is not weakness; it is wisdom. The willingness to be wrong makes the team brave enough to be honest.

Leadership resistance also grows from the illusion that control equals stability. When leaders tighten control, they suppress creativity and feedback—two elements essential to innovation. Control feels safe but leads to stagnation. Connection feels risky but produces growth.

A leader's ability to tolerate discomfort determines the team's capacity for change. When leaders let go of the need to control every outcome, they invite collaboration. When they release ego, they make space for trust. Leadership is not about holding power tightly; it is about holding people safely.

Resistance reveals what leaders need to learn about themselves. Each moment of pushback invites reflection:

> ⇒ What am I protecting right now, progress or pride?

> ⇒ What emotion is showing up for me as I face resistance?

> ⇒ What truth might I be avoiding?

The leader who asks these questions transforms resistance from frustration into feedback. Resistance does not just test leadership; it *teaches* it.

These three forms of resistance rarely appear in isolation. They overlap and reinforce one another. A human fear can trigger systemic barriers, which then amplify leadership defensiveness. That cycle can quietly derail entire initiatives.

The key is awareness. Leaders who recognize resistance in all its layers can respond with nuance:

> ⇒ Empathy for the human.

> ⇒ Redesign for the system.

> ⇒ Reflection for themselves.

That is how change becomes collaborative instead of combative. When resistance is met eye to eye, not with judgment but with curiosity, it transforms from a wall into a window. Resistance does not block the path; it becomes the path that leads to deeper understanding.

Leaders who meet resistance with empathy and honesty turn tension into trust. They do not ignore discomfort; they *engage* it. The strength of a leader is not measured by how they avoid resistance but by how they *face* it.

The following four practices: *Recognize, Reflect, Respond, and Rebuild,* form a framework for turning resistance into relationship. These are not steps to control others but principles to connect with them.

1. Recognize: Name What You Notice

The first practice of meeting resistance eye to eye is *recognition.* Leaders cannot address what they refuse to see.

Recognition begins when leaders notice subtle signs such as a shift in tone, silence in meetings, or a pattern of avoidance. Instead of labeling those moments as defiance, they pause and ask, *"What might this be telling me?"*

Recognition turns reaction into reflection. By naming resistance early, leaders reduce its power. They bring it into the open, where dialogue can replace assumption.

What we name, we can navigate. What we ignore, we repeat.

Leadership Practices for Recognition:

⇒ Observe behavior without judgment.

⇒ Use neutral language: "I sense some hesitation. Can we talk about what is behind it?"

⇒ Avoid diagnosing emotion ("You're resistant") and focus on describing impact: "I notice we have not moved forward yet. Help me understand why."

Recognition is not confrontation. It is curiosity.

2. Reflect: Listen Beneath the Surface

Once resistance is named, reflection begins. Reflection is the art of *listening beneath the words* and hearing emotion, not just explanation.

When people resist, they are rarely saying "no" to the leader. They are saying "no" to something that feels unsafe or unclear.

The reflective leader does not rush to defend. They hold space and ask questions that open trust.

> ⇒ "What are you protecting right now?"

> ⇒ "What would make this easier?"

> ⇒ "What do you need to feel ready?"

These questions turn conflict into collaboration. Reflection turns resistance from argument into awareness.

Leadership Practices for Reflection

> ⇒ Repeat what you hear to confirm understanding: "It sounds like you are concerned about losing autonomy. Is that right?"

> ⇒ Validate emotion without agreeing or disagreeing.

⇒ Reflect not only on others' resistance but also on your own: "What is being triggered in me right now?"

Reflection slows down reaction long enough for empathy to catch up.

3. Respond: Lead with Empathy and Boundaries

Once resistance is understood, respond with balance through empathy *and* boundaries.

Empathy without direction leads to confusion. Direction without empathy breeds resentment. The leader's strength lies in holding both.

A good response does not force compliance. It builds commitment.

Responding with empathy might sound like:

⇒ "I understand this feels uncertain. Let's take it one step at a time."

⇒ "You have raised valid concerns. Here is what we can adapt, and here is what must stay the same."

⇒ "I appreciate your honesty. Let's co-create a plan that works for both of us."

Boundaries do not cancel empathy. They protect it. Leaders who respond clearly prevent resistance from hardening into rebellion.

Empathy without boundaries leads to exhaustion. Boundaries without empathy become barriers.

Leadership Practices for Response

⇒ Communicate next steps simply and clearly.

⇒ Provide choice where possible, since autonomy reduces defensiveness.

⇒ Acknowledge limits honestly: "Here is what I can do, and here is what I cannot."

Responding this way turns resistance into dialogue instead of debate.

4. Rebuild: Transform Resistance into Relationship

Rebuilding is the stage where healing begins and trust grows back stronger than before.

When resistance is met instead of ignored, something powerful happens: people feel seen. Being seen rebuilds belonging.

Rebuilding does not mean pretending nothing happened. It means integrating the experience into new understanding. A team that has faced resistance together becomes more resilient. They know they can face discomfort and still remain connected.

Rebuilding is also where leaders model vulnerability by admitting what they have learned through the process.

⇒ "I realize I could have communicated that better."

⇒ "Your feedback helped me see things differently."

⇒ "Thank you for pushing back. It made our plan stronger."

These moments turn authority into authenticity.

The leader who listens builds bridges that last longer than any plan.

Leadership Practices for Rebuilding

⇒ Celebrate honesty and courage.

⇒ Follow up after difficult conversations to show continuity.

⇒ Record lessons learned and make them part of the system's

⇒ evolution.

Rebuilding proves that connection is stronger than conflict.

When Resistance Becomes Relationship

When leaders move through all four practices: Recognize, Reflect, Respond, and Rebuild, resistance stops being an interruption and becomes an initiation.

It marks the moment when leadership shifts from *managing behavior to understanding emotion.* The energy that once blocked progress becomes the energy that drives it. The same people who resisted the hardest often become the strongest advocates because they were given the dignity of being heard. The goal is not to end resistance. The goal is to earn relationship. But even with the best systems in place, leaders must remember that change still meets human emotion. Resistance is not always defiance; often, it is protection; protection of what is familiar, predictable, or previously safe.

When people push back, they are not resisting the leader; they are resisting the loss of what they have known. When leaders learn to read that resistance with empathy and precision, they unlock a deeper understanding of how to guide their teams forward.

Which brings us to the framework that helps leaders engage with resistance in a more intentional, human-centered way.

Framework Summary: Meeting Resistance Eye to Eye

Practice	Focus	Outcome	Leadership Example
Recognize	Notice and name resistance early	Awareness	"I sense some hesitation; can we explore it together?"
Reflect	Listen for emotion beneath the surface	Empathy	"It sounds like you're protecting something important tell me more."
Respond	Balance empathy with boundaries	Direction	"Here's what we can change; here's what stays constant."

Practice	Focus	Outcome	Leadership Example
Rebuild	Transform conflict into connection	Trust	"Thank you for pushing back this made our work stronger."

This cycle does more than defuse tension; it develops emotional intelligence across the organization.

When leaders model how to meet resistance, they teach their teams how to handle conflict with compassion. They normalize dialogue instead of defensiveness. Over time, that normalization becomes culture.

True cultural strength is not built in moments of agreement but in moments of understanding. Each time resistance is met with curiosity instead of control, the organization grows more resilient, more connected, and more human.

Reflection Prompts

1. What does resistance usually trigger in me: frustration, fear, or curiosity?

2. How do I typically respond when my ideas are challenged?

3. When have I interpreted resistance as disrespect instead of emotion?

4. What systems around me might unintentionally reinforce old habits?

5. How can I use the four practices: Recognize, Reflect, Respond, and Rebuild, in a current challenge I am facing?

Pull Quotes for Design

"Resistance isn't rejection; it's protection."

"People don't resist facts; they resist disconnection."

"What we name, we can navigate. What we ignore, we repeat."

"Empathy without boundaries is exhaustion. Boundaries without empathy are walls."

"The goal is not to end resistance; it's to earn relationship."

"The leader who listens builds bridges that last longer than any plan."

Closing Reflection: Eye to Eye

Resistance, at its core, is an invitation, not an interruption. It invites leaders to slow down, listen more deeply, and see people not as problems to fix but as partners to understand.

When we meet resistance eye to eye, we look past fear and find humanity. We discover that the very emotions we once tried to avoid: discomfort, disagreement, and doubt, are the ones that deepen connection and strengthen trust.

Leaders who learn this no longer fear resistance. They *expect* it, welcome it, and use it to refine their approach. Resistance, when met with empathy and courage, becomes the birthplace of belonging.

Change without resistance is compliance. Change with conversation becomes commitment.

10

EMBEDDING CHANGE IN PEOPLE'S

STORIES

T he project looked like a success on paper. Deadlines were met, the technology was deployed, and workflows were redesigned. At the closing ceremony the leader smiled with genuine pride. Months of work had paid off. She listed the milestones, thanked contributors, and closed with, "We did it." Everyone applauded and then moved on to the next assignment.

A few months later she noticed something strange. Old habits were quietly returning. The new tools were not being used. The same communication silos were creeping back in. She asked a colleague, "Did not we agree to use the new process?" He shrugged and said, "Oh, that? I guess we just went back to what we know."

It was not resistance. It was forgetfulness. The change had not failed, it had faded. The initiative lived in documents and data, but not in daily conversations, values, or memories. Change that does not live in people's stories dies in their routines. The leader realized she had communicated the *strategy*, not cultivated the *story*. She had explained the what and the how, but not the why that creates ownership. Facts inform, but stories transform. Stories turn change into meaning, and meaning endures.

Humans are storytelling creatures. Long before policies or spreadsheets existed, we made sense of life through stories of survival, belonging, and hope. Every time people experience change, their minds try to fit it into a narrative:

⇒ *What's happening?*

⇒ *How does this affect me?*

⇒ *Am I the hero, the helper, or the one left behind?*

When change feels imposed, people feel like background characters in someone else's story. When they understand their role and the meaning behind it, they become co-authors. Successful change is not just managed, it is *storied.* Leaders who embed change in narrative help people connect the past they knew, the present they are navigating, and the future they are building. People do not buy into change; they buy into the story that explains why the change matters.

The anatomy of story-driven change weaves three universal human needs:

1. **Coherence** The need for the story to make sense.

2. **Belonging** The need to see ourselves in the story.

3. **Purpose** The need to believe the story matters.

Without these, change feels chaotic, isolating, or meaningless. When they are present, people do more than adapt; they align.

1.   **Coherence The need to make sense**

Change disrupts the familiar patterns our minds use for stability. When the story feels disjointed, people experience cognitive dissonance. One of the first questions during any change is, *"Why now?"* Leaders who tell coherent stories build a bridge from what was to what will be. Coherence does not mean everything is perfect. It means people can understand *how things fit together*.

For example, a school introducing a new learning model might say, "For years we focused on content mastery. Now we will expand to creativity and problem solving because the world our students are entering demands it." That sentence gives change a timeline and therefore, coherence.

2. **Belonging The need to be seen**

    Every change story must answer one emotional question: *Where do I fit?* When change is communicated impersonally, people feel erased. When leaders make space for individual and collective voices, people feel valued. Belonging happens when the story includes *us*, not just *them*.

    Inclusive storytelling changes passive observers into active participants. Without belonging, people may comply but never commit.

3. **Purpose The need to matter**

    Purpose transforms endurance into engagement. It gives effort meaning and struggle dignity. When leaders connect daily tasks to a higher purpose, they awaken intrinsic motivation. A healthcare organization might remind staff, "Every new process we adopt helps one more patient feel safe and cared for." That sentence anchors the change to human impact. Purpose turns "another initiative" into "our shared mission."

Organizations often invest in *change management plans:* timelines, deliverables, checklists, but few invest in *meaning management*, the narrative that generates ownership. When story is missing, three predictable patterns emerge:

1. **Disconnection**: people do not see themselves in the change.

2. **Disbelief:** they do not understand *why* it is happening.

3. **Drift:** once the project ends, old habits quietly return.

The leader in the opening story did not fail strategically; she failed narratively. She changed the system but not the story that lived inside people's hearts. Change without story is movement without memory.

Embedding change in people's stories means moving beyond announcements toward integration. Announcements tell. Embedding transforms. To embed change, leaders should:

⇒ **Connect new ideas to existing identity:** "This is who we are, evolving."

⇒ **Create language people can repeat:** a simple phrase that captures what you are doing.

⇒ **Celebrate small wins publicly:** show progress as shared history.

⇒ **Invite storytelling from every level:** ask, "What has this change meant for you?"

When people start repeating the new story in their own words, the change has taken root. It no longer belongs to the leader; it belongs to *the culture.*

The Story Beneath Every Change

Every change tells a deeper story:

> ⇒ A story of growth *We are becoming something bigger.*

> ⇒ A story of healing *We are repairing what was broken.*

> ⇒ A story of courage *We are stepping into the unknown together.*

Leaders who articulate that deeper narrative give people emotional oxygen. They help teams see change not as loss but as legacy in motion. When people see themselves in the story, they stop fearing the ending and start writing the next chapter.

Every change begins inside the story we tell ourselves. When people face transformation: a new role, a new system, a new identity, they unconsciously start rewriting their inner narrative:

> ⇒ *Who am I in this new reality?*

> ⇒ *What am I losing?*

> ⇒ *What am I learning?*

This personal story is where resistance often hides. Resistance is not always in the policy or the process; it lives in the quiet space between *who I was* and *who I must now become*. For some, that space felt exciting. For others, it felt like loss. Change asked people to update not just their behavior, but their biography.

When leaders understood this, they stopped asking, *"Why are people resisting?"* and started asking, *"What identity are they protecting?"* Change was personal before it was organizational.

During transformation, people experienced *a narrative gap*, a temporary loss of coherence between their past and future selves. In that gap they said things like:

> ⇒ "This is not how we have always done it."

> ⇒ "I just do not feel like myself anymore."

> ⇒ "Everything I knew how to do does not seem to matter now."

These were not restatements of defiance but expressions of disorientation. Leaders who rushed to correct them missed a chance to connect.

By asking, "What part of this change feels hardest to explain to yourself?" leaders invited people to process meaning instead of defending identity. Once people began integrating change into their self-story, seeing how it aligned with their strengths, values, or aspirations, adaptation accelerated.

This shift matters. People do not resist change itself; they resist the story they believe the change will force them to live. When leaders help them reinterpret that story, the emotional weight begins to lift. What once felt like a threat becomes an evolution. What once triggered withdrawal now sparks curiosity.

Effective leaders understand that change never starts with logistics; it starts with language. The words people use to describe their discomfort are windows into their inner world. When leaders listen without rushing to fix, they discover the emotional truth beneath the surface,the fear of irrelevance, the worry of being misunderstood, the uncertainty of losing competence, community, or control.

The most powerful thing a leader could do was help someone reframe their story. Examples:

⇒ From *"I am losing control"* to *"I am learning to lead differently."*

⇒ From *"I am being replaced by technology"* to *"I am evolving my expertise."*

⇒ From *"My past work does not matter"* to *"My experience built the foundation for this new chapter."*

Reframing was not denial, it was integration. It allowed people to carry their history forward with dignity. People did not need an entirely new story; they needed help finding themselves in the new story. When leaders affirmed someone's value during transition, they gave that person permission to belong in the future.

While the personal story defined individual meaning, the team story defined *collective identity*. Teams, like people, needed coherence, belonging, and purpose. Without a shared story, collaboration became coordination, transactional instead of transformational. Teams began saying, "We are busy," instead of, "We are becoming."

A strong team story answered three questions:

1. **Who are we?** (Identity)

2. **Why do we matter?** (Purpose)

3. **Where are we going together?** (Direction)

When those questions were answered collectively, alignment followed. Language was how teams held their story together. Think of a sports team, a school faculty, or a small business, each has phrases, symbols, or rituals that communicate belonging. The same principle applied to change. Teams that co-created their language created ownership.

Examples:

⇒ A corporate team might say, *"We are building smarter, not faster."*

⇒ A school might say, *"Every classroom, every child, every day."*

⇒ A nonprofit might say, *"From charity to change."*

Those phrases acted as narrative anchors. They reminded everyone of what they were doing *together*. Shared language built shared identity. When teams repeated their story in meetings, emails, and celebrations, they reinforced meaning through rhythm.

Change began to sound familiar, and familiarity bred trust. Teams needed moments that reminded them they were progressing. Milestones were not just metrics, they were emotional markers that said, *"We are still moving forward."*

Every milestone, big or small, added a new sentence to the team's collective story:

> ⇒ "Remember when we did not think we could hit that goal?"

> ⇒ "Remember when we finally got everyone on board?"

> ⇒ "Remember when we saw our idea come to life?"

By revisiting these memories together, leaders strengthened continuity, the sense that *past effort mattered to future progress.* When change became a story of shared achievement, it became something people were proud to remember.

Organizations were, at their core, story systems. Policies, procedures, and strategies mattered, but they were all shaped by the stories people told about what success looked like, who belonged, and what behavior got rewarded. To embed change into culture, leaders had to rewrite the organizational story, not through slogans but through *symbols, rituals, and recognition.* Culture was the story people told when leaders were not in the room.

When old stories lingered, "That is just how we have always done it," or "We tried that before and it failed", they became barriers to transformation. Leaders had to replace inherited narratives with living ones that connected past values to future purpose. Change stuck when it honored continuity. Instead of discarding the past, wise leaders wove it into the new story. For example, rather than saying, *"We are not the same company we used to be,"* they might say, "We are building on our legacy of excellence and redefining it for what comes next." That phrasing acknowledged identity while inviting evolution. It told people: *you are not being replaced, you are being reimagined.* Change without continuity created cultural amnesia, and amnesia killed belonging.

Continuity kept memory alive while making room for momentum. Stories survived through ritual. In education, morning meetings set tone. In organizations, team check-ins, storytelling sessions, or recognition events embedded meaning. Rituals turned intention into habit. They made the story *tangible.*

Examples of rituals that reinforced story:

$\Rightarrow$ Start team meetings with a "story of progress."

$\Rightarrow$ End the week with a reflection on what was learned.

⇒ Create symbolic milestones, like naming a project room after a value: ("The Courage Room" or "The Bridge Lab.")

Each ritual whispered the story of the culture. When those rituals aligned with the change narrative, the story became self-sustaining. Rituals were how organizations remembered who they were.

When personal, team, and organizational stories aligned, change became identity.

⇒ The **individual** said, *"This is who I am becoming."*

⇒ The **team** said, *"This is who we are together."*

⇒ The **organization** said, *"This is what we stand for."*

That alignment created coherence, the emotional glue that kept transformation alive long after the project ended. It was not compliance, it was community. Change lasted when it became part of how people described themselves. The beauty of story-driven change was that it scaled without force because people naturally shared stories that felt true, proud, and personal. When they told the story in their own words, the change had truly taken root. Stories were the vessels that carried culture. They reminded people who they were, what they valued, and where they were going.

When change succeeded, it was because leaders embedded it into these stories, not as a temporary campaign but as a living narrative that evolved over time. Across hundreds of transformations, from classrooms to corporations, four consistent layers emerged whenever change truly took root. Together, they formed the *Four Layers of Story-Driven Change: Identity, Meaning, Memory, and Momentum.*

1. **Identity Who we were becoming**

Every story began with identity. Change threatened it at first; people wondered, *"Who am I in this new version of us?"* Leaders who ignored that question lost trust. Leaders who embraced it built resilience. Identity answered the who of change, both individually and collectively. When leaders framed transformation as *evolution* instead of *erasure,* people could see continuity between their past selves and their future potential.

For example, rather than saying,
"We are moving away from how we have always done things,"
a leader might say,
"We are building on our strengths and stretching into new skills."
That shift acknowledged pride while inviting progress.
Change that threatened identity met resistance. Change that evolved identity inspired pride.

Leadership practices for identity

> ⇒ Connect change to values and strengths already present.

> ⇒ Celebrate who people are *as much* as who they are becoming.

> ⇒ Ask, "What parts of our identity are essential to carry forward?"

When identity was honored, change felt like continuity, not crisis.

2. **Meaning Why it mattered**

The second layer was meaning, the why behind the work. Meaning transformed compliance into commitment. It turned routine into relevance. People could tolerate uncertainty when they understood purpose. When meaning was missing, even small changes felt heavy.

Leaders embedded meaning by connecting transformation to human impact:

> ⇒ "This is not just about efficiency; it is about freeing time for what matters most."

> ⇒ "This update helps every student, patient, or customer feel seen."

> ⇒ Meaning made the abstract personal. It linked strategy to emotion.

Leadership practices for meaning

⇒ Start every communication *with why it matters before what changes.*

⇒ Tell stories of impact, not just improvement.

⇒ Invite others to share what gives the change meaning for them.

Meaning was not assigned from the top. It was discovered through conversation.

3. Memory How we honored the past

The third layer was memory, the continuity thread that kept culture grounded. Too often organizations treated the past like a problem to erase. People needed to know that their history still mattered. When leaders honored memory, they created space for nostalgia and pride, not shame. Acknowledging what came before did not slow progress, it fueled it.

Examples of honoring memory during change

⇒ "This new chapter builds on the foundation you helped create."

⇒ "We could not take this step without the lessons of where we have been."

⇒ "Let us carry forward what worked and release what no longer serves us."

Memory humanized momentum and rooted growth in gratitude.

Leadership practices for memory

⇒ Celebrate legacy moments in change rollouts.

⇒ Document stories of how you got here.

⇒ Involve long-tenured employees in shaping the narrative.

Memory gave people the dignity of continuity, and continuity kept culture emotionally intact.

4. **Momentum How we moved forward together**

The final layer was momentum, the living energy that kept the story alive. Momentum was not about speed; it was about direction. It was sustained through rhythm: rituals, reflection, and reminders that progress was still unfolding. When change slowed or fatigue set in, leaders rekindled momentum by returning to story: "Remember where we started? Look how far we have come."

Momentum was built one story at a time. When people retold moments of progress, they reinforced confidence for individuals and the team.

Leadership practices for momentum

> ⇒ Regularly revisit milestones as shared victories.

> ⇒ Keep language consistent over time, for example, "We are still becoming."

> ⇒ Encourage everyone to share new stories that reflect ongoing growth.

Momentum ensured that change did not end with a rollout. It became a living rhythm inside the culture's story.

Framework Summary: The Four Layers of Story Driven Change

Layer	Focus	Emotional Need	Leadership Action
Identity	Who we are becoming	Pride and continuity	Connect change to existing strengths and values
Meaning	Why it	Purpose	Link transformation to

Layer	Focus	Emotional Need	Leadership Action
Identity	Matters	and Direction	Human Impact
Memory	How we honor the past	Gratitude and belonging	Acknowledge history and legacy openly
Momentum	How we move forward together	Hope and progress	Keep revisiting and retelling the evolving story

Together, these layers turn change from a project into a narrative. When leaders integrate all four, people stop asking, "When will this be over?" and start saying, "This is who we are now."

That shift from event to identity is the ultimate goal of embedded change.

Reflection prompts

1. What story do people in my organization talk about our last major change? Does it inspire pride or pain?

2. How do I honor the past while inviting the future?

3. What part of our identity is evolving, and what part must remain constant?

4. How can I help others find their own story within this change?

5. What rituals or reminders could keep our story alive long after the project ends?

Pull quotes for layout design

"Change that does not live in people's stories dies in their routines."

"People do not need a new story; they need help finding themselves in the new story."

"Culture is the story people tell when leaders are not in the room."

"You cannot move forward if people feel they have to forget where they came from."

"Momentum grows where meaning meets memory."

"When people tell the story in their own words, the change has taken root."

Closing reflection When change becomes story

Change lasts when it feels like a story people want to tell.

Not a mandate. Not a project. A story, one that makes them proud to say, *"I was part of that."*

When leaders embed change into people's stories, they transform it from compliance into connection. They honor the past, clarify the purpose, and give people a future worth remembering. The result is more than transformation; it is transcendence. Because when change becomes story, it becomes legacy. And legacy is not what leaders build *for* people; it is what they build *with* them.

"Strategy changes systems. Story changes souls."

11

MEASURING THE FACES OF CHANGE

The report that missed the real success

The report was immaculate.

Charts lined up, metrics told a tidy story, and the executive summary checked every box. After months of leading a large-scale transformation, the leader proudly presented her final evaluation. The numbers looked good:

⇒ Productivity was up 12 percent.

⇒ Customer satisfaction increased 9 percent.

⇒ Turnover dropped slightly.

From a technical standpoint, the project was a success. But when she looked around the room during her presentation, something did not sit right. The people who had done the work: the ones who had stayed late, coached peers, or quietly held morale together, were not smiling. They were tired.

When she asked, "How do you feel about everything we accomplished?" the room fell silent. Finally, one person said softly, "I guess we did what we had to do."

That moment changed her understanding of success. The numbers were correct, but incomplete. They showed *what happened,* not what *it meant*. The true story of change was not in the charts. It lived in conversations, in trust rebuilt, in courage shown, and in humanity rediscovered. Those things were not captured in her report because she had not measured them.

Data tells us what moved. Story tells us what mattered.

From that day forward she decided that no future report would be considered complete until it included the human experience behind the numbers. That decision marked her evolution from managing outcomes to measuring transformation.

Why measurement needs a human face

Measurement is not just a technical process. It is a moral one. What leaders choose to measure communicates what they value. What they fail to measure reveals what they overlook.

When organizations measure only efficiency, they lose sight of empathy. When they measure only speed, they ignore sustainability. When they measure only profit, they forget people.

The best leaders redefine measurement as a form of *visibility*. Measurement is not about proving success; it is about *seeing fully*, the outcomes, the obstacles, and the emotional journey in between.

What gets measured gets managed, but what gets felt gets remembered.

To measure change effectively, leaders must look beyond metrics of movement toward metrics of meaning. They must measure not only what changed, but *who changed and how*.

The human side of measurement

Every transformation has two parallel dimensions:

1. The **operational**: what processes, systems, or behaviors shifted.

2. The **emotional**: how people experienced that shift.

Most leaders are trained to measure the first. Few are equipped to measure the second. Yet the emotional and relational impact determines whether the change endures. People might comply with a new system because they have to, but they will only *sustain* it if they believe in it. That belief cannot be forced; it must be *felt*. What people feel must be intentionally measured.

Quantifying the qualitative

The challenge is not that human factors cannot be measured. The challenge is that we have been taught to call them soft. Trust, belonging, morale, and psychological safety may sound intangible, but they have real, measurable indicators.

For example:

> ⇒ **Trust** can be tracked through pulse surveys, participation in open feedback, and peer-to-peer recognition rates.

> ⇒ **Belonging** can be measured by engagement, retention, and inclusion sentiment.

> ⇒ **Morale** shows up in discretionary effort, creativity, and the willingness to take initiative.

When organizations begin to quantify these so-called soft measures, they discover that what is soft actually holds everything together. The human side of measurement is not emotion versus evidence. It is emotion as evidence.

Measuring what people experience

Imagine two teams completing the same project. Team A finished faster. Team B finished slower but reported higher trust, clearer communication, and better cross-department collaboration. Which one created sustainable change?

Most organizations would reward Team A. Six months later, Team B was still thriving because they built relationships, not just results. The best measurement systems look at both *efficiency* and *experience.*

Leaders who evaluate change holistically ask:

⇒ How did this process impact people's energy, trust, and

confidence?

⇒ Did communication feel clear and inclusive?

⇒ What behaviors or beliefs are different now than when we began?

These questions uncover the real story behind success.

The ethics of measurement

Measurement is not neutral. It shapes behavior. When leaders measure only output, people learn to hide fatigue. When they measure only compliance, people stop taking risks. When they measure only performance, they sacrifice presence.

When leaders measure well-being, learning, and engagement alongside results, people align action with authenticity. Measurement becomes a mirror, not a microscope. It reflects the health of both the system and the soul. Measurement should serve people, not pressure them.

Ethical measurement ensures that data collection does not dehumanize the people who made progress possible. It emphasizes inquiry over inspection and curiosity over control. Leaders who practice ethical measurement ask, "What story are our numbers telling, and whose voice is missing from it?"

The story beneath the data

Data is the skeleton of progress. Story is its heartbeat. When leaders integrate both, they create evaluation systems that feel alive, not mechanical.

Consider how this looks in practice:

> ⇒ A *corporate* team collects quarterly engagement data and then holds story circles where employees share what is improving or fading.

> ⇒ A *school* district measures teacher retention alongside stories of classroom innovation.

⇒ A nonprofit tracks community outcomes and invites participants to describe how programs changed their lives.

These narratives enrich the data with empathy and depth. Numbers without stories are hollow. Stories without numbers are hard to scale. Together they form evidence with soul. Data reveals the what. Stories reveal the why. Both are required for truth.

The courage to see what is really there

Measuring change means being willing to see the whole picture, even when it is uncomfortable. True measurement does not only celebrate success. It reveals friction, fatigue, and failure as opportunities to learn.

This requires emotional courage. It is easier to present perfect metrics than to admit that progress is uneven or that morale dipped during transition. Honest measurement creates trust because it mirrors reality.

Leaders who are brave enough to see, name, and learn from the full story create cultures of transparency and growth. That is how measurement evolves from accountability to *integrity.*

Leadership maturity shows up not in the metrics we present, but in the truths, we are willing to face.

The Cultural Lens: Measuring What People Live and Feel

Culture is not a poster on the wall; it is the pattern of behavior people repeat when no one is watching. It shows up in how meetings feel, how feedback is handled, how leaders respond to mistakes, and how trust is built or broken. Because culture is lived, not declared, it must be *observed, listened to, and measured* through experience.

"Culture is what people remember feeling, not what leaders remember saying."

The cultural lens of measurement invites leaders to look for emotional evidence: the subtle, human signals that reveal whether change is thriving or merely surviving.

Listening as a Cultural Metric

The first indicator of a healthy culture is not compliance; it is *conversation*. When people feel safe to speak up, ask questions, and disagree respectfully, change becomes collaborative. When silence grows, disengagement follows.

Listening can be measured. Leaders can track:

⇒ Response rates to surveys and open-ended questions

⇒ Participation in feedback sessions or retrospectives

⇒ Diversity of voices represented in discussions

⇒ Sentiment analysis from pulse checks or town halls

These data points reveal psychological safety, the foundation of trust. "The loudest silence in any organization is the one after a difficult question."

If no one is asking hard questions, the culture may not be ready for real growth.

Belonging as an Outcome

Every major change process affects belonging. It either strengthens inclusion or exposes who feels left out.

Belonging can be measured not by attendance, but by emotional participation:

⇒ Do people feel seen and valued in the change process?

⇒ Are different perspectives invited into decision-making?

⇒ Does recognition reach beyond the usual voices?

Simple indicators such as peer recognition frequency, participation in optional initiatives, or tone in internal communication can offer valuable insight.

Belonging is not abstract; it is measurable through the consistency of inclusion.

"Belonging is not about fitting in. It is about feeling safe enough to stand out."

Storytelling as a Cultural Barometer

One of the most underused tools in evaluation is story. The stories people tell inside an organization reveal what the culture truly believes.

After major change, listen for how people describe it:

⇒ Are they saying, "We survived it"?

⇒ Or are they saying, "We grew through it"?

Those small differences in language show whether transformation has been internalized. Conducting story audits by gathering short reflections from staff, clients, or partners helps leaders understand the emotional temperature of their culture. The stories people share spontaneously are often the truest measure of morale.

"Numbers count what happened. Stories explain why people cared."

The Organizational Lens: Aligning Systems with Purpose

Once leaders understand what people are *feeling*, the next step is to measure what the *system* is reinforcing. Organizations often track outcomes without realizing their structures reward the wrong behaviors.

For example:

⇒ Measuring individual productivity while preaching teamwork

⇒ Measuring short-term results while claiming to value sustainability

⇒ Measuring activity while ignoring actual impact

If systems do not align with stated values, resistance grows and trust erodes. Organizational measurement must go beyond performance to purpose, ensuring metrics reflect not only what was achieved but also *how* it was achieved.

"The way we measure success defines the kind of success we create."

From Output to Outcome

Most organizations track *outputs*: things produced, tasks completed, dollars saved. Transformational leadership measures *outcomes*, the change created because of those outputs.

Output says: "We trained 300 employees."
Outcome says: "Eighty percent now report greater confidence and collaboration."

The difference is meaning. Outcome measurement connects effort to experience and confirms that behavior has truly shifted. It is not just checking if people showed up; it is checking if they *changed.*

Integrating Quantitative and Qualitative Metrics

True evaluation blends numbers and narratives. It uses surveys *and* storytelling, dashboards *and* dialogue.

An organizational measurement framework might include:

⇒ **Quantitative metrics:** performance data, attendance, retention, customer satisfaction, speed of adoption

⇒ **Qualitative metrics:** interviews, focus groups, open-text survey responses, reflection journals

Together, they create a 360-degree view of change.

In practice, this might look like:

⇒ A school measuring both student outcomes *and* teacher morale

⇒ A hospital tracking patient satisfaction alongside staff resilience

⇒ A nonprofit evaluating community impact *and* volunteer engagement

Each combination tells the full story, the metrics and the meaning intertwined. "Data without humanity is directionless. Humanity without data is ungrounded."

The Power of Behavioral Indicators

Another powerful way to measure organizational change is through *behavior*. Instead of asking only how people feel, look at what they do *differently*.

Examples include:

⇒ Increased collaboration across departments

⇒ Faster problem resolution without escalation

⇒ Greater initiative and accountability

⇒ Lower absenteeism or burnout reports

These behaviors signal that the culture is absorbing change at a deeper level, that the system is adapting, not just adjusting. Behavioral data bridges emotional progress and operational performance. It proves that transformation is not only being discussed; it is being *demonstrated.*

Evaluating Leadership Behavior

Since culture mirrors leadership, measuring leaders' own behaviors is essential.

Ask:

⇒ How consistently do leaders model the organization's stated values?

⇒ Do employees perceive fairness and transparency in decisions?

⇒ How often do leaders seek and act on feedback?

Leadership effectiveness surveys, 360-degree evaluations, and coaching reflections can reveal patterns between leader behavior and team morale.

When leaders are evaluated not only on *what* they deliver but also on *how* they lead, accountability deepens.

"The culture of measurement must start with the people who create it."

If leaders are not modeling curiosity, empathy, and transparency, no metric will make up for that absence.

Systems That Measure What Matters

The most successful organizations design evaluation systems that are:

1. **Aligned:** Metrics mirror mission and values.

2. **Balanced:** Quantitative and qualitative data complement each other.

3. **Accessible:** Data is shared transparently to build trust.

4. **Actionable:** Findings lead to learning, not punishment.

When systems meet these four conditions, measurement becomes part of culture, not a compliance exercise. People stop asking, "What is being measured?" and start asking, "What is being learned?"

"Measurement should open conversations, not close them."

When people feel ownership of the data, they use it as a tool for progress, not as a source of anxiety. That is when numbers start telling *human* stories.

Case Insight: When Data Meets Dignity

In one global organization, leaders introduced a "well-being dashboard" alongside performance metrics. Each month, teams anonymously reported on:

⇒ Workload balance

⇒ Psychological safety

⇒ Sense of belonging

⇒ Energy level

Initially, leaders feared the results would be too subjective. But within six months, departments using the dashboard showed *higher performance and lower turnover* than those that did not.

Why? Because measurement had become a conversation, not a report card.

By treating humanity as measurable, the organization redefined success as something *sustainable*.

"When you measure what matters to people, people give their best to what matters."

The Four Measures of Visible Change

Measurement is not about perfection. It is about perception, participation, performance, and persistence.
When leaders learn to track these four dimensions, they stop chasing quick wins and start cultivating *lasting alignment*.
These measures do not only evaluate what has changed; they reveal *how deeply* the change has taken root.

1. Perception: What People Feel and Believe

Perception is the most immediate and emotional layer of measurement.
It answers the question, *"How does this change feel?"*

This is not about vanity metrics or popularity contests. It is about gauging whether people understand, trust, and believe in the purpose behind transformation. When perception is positive, people interpret change as opportunity. When perception is negative, even good initiatives can feel threatening.

Perception can be measured through:

⇒ Pulse surveys and listening sessions

⇒ Open text feedback analysis

⇒ Sentiment tracking in meetings, chat channels, or communities of practice

⇒ Storytelling audits that collect short reflections from employees or stakeholders

These tools reveal how people *make sense* of change, the emotional narrative forming beneath the surface.

"Perception shapes participation. People act on the story they believe, not the plan they read."

Leadership Practices for Measuring Perception:

⇒ Ask: "What emotions are present in our change conversations?"

⇒ Use qualitative check-ins before and after milestones.

⇒ Share perception findings transparently; people trust leaders who do not hide discomfort.

When perception is seen as data, emotion becomes insight.

2. Participation: What People Do and Contribute

Participation shows how deeply people are engaging with the change, whether they are merely complying or genuinely collaborating.

This measure answers the question: *"Who is showing up, and how?"*

Participation is both quantitative and behavioral. It includes:

⇒ Attendance at training or dialogue sessions

⇒ Volunteerism in change committees or pilot programs

⇒ Frequency of feedback submissions

⇒ Visible ownership of new practices

But participation also has an emotional side. It is not just about showing up; it is about showing up wholeheartedly.
The quality of participation reflects the quality of trust.

"Participation is the bridge between belief and behavior."

Leadership Practices for Measuring Participation:

⇒ Track engagement across levels, not just volume.

⇒ Celebrate contributors publicly to normalize ownership.

⇒ Ask: "Who is not in the room yet, and why?"

If participation is uneven, the story of change is incomplete.

3. Performance: What Results Are Emerging

Performance remains essential, but it is now part of a larger picture. It asks: *"What is actually improving?"*

Performance measurement becomes powerful when it blends operational and relational indicators.
That means tracking not only *what changed*, such as productivity, efficiency, and outcomes, but also *how people experienced the journey*, including collaboration, communication, and psychological safety.

In a healthy system, both rise together.

For example:

⇒ An organization with high innovation scores should also show improved morale.

⇒ A school raising academic outcomes should also track student belonging.

⇒ A company hitting revenue targets should also sustain engagement levels.

When performance improves at the cost of well-being, it is not progress; it is depletion.

"Performance without humanity is short lived. Humanity without performance is un-sustained."

Leadership Practices for Measuring Performance:

⇒ Integrate well-being metrics into key performance indicators.

⇒ Evaluate leadership behavior alongside outcomes.

⇒ Link each success measure to its corresponding human factor, such as innovation to psychological safety.

When performance reflects both achievement and alignment, success becomes sustainable.

4. Persistence: What Endures After the Spotlight Fades

Persistence is the ultimate measure, the proof that change has become culture.

It asks: *"What remains when no one is measuring?"*

Sustainability cannot be seen in the first month after rollout; it appears in the quiet consistency that follows.

Persistence is about habit, language, and legacy.

It is when people use new systems naturally, when leaders reference values without prompting, when the story of change becomes "just the way we do things now."

Persistence can be tracked through:

⇒ Long term data, six to twelve months after implementation

⇒ Continued alignment in feedback and performance metrics

⇒ Retention of shared language or rituals

⇒ New innovations emerging *because* of the change

"The truest sign of transformation is continuity, when new habits outlast the initiative that created them."

Leadership Practices for Measuring Persistence:

⇒ Schedule post change evaluations at regular intervals.

⇒ Ask: "What part of this feels natural now, and what still feels forced?"

⇒ Encourage teams to tell stories about what has lasted.

But measurement is not just about checking progress it is about noticing patterns. Leaders who listen for what people repeat, reference, or rely on begin to see which behaviors have taken root and which ones never found soil.

Persistence reveals itself in the quiet moments: in the habits that no longer require reminders, in the language teams use without prompting, and in the decisions people make when no one is watching.

Leaders should also look for signs of drift. When old behaviors begin resurfacing, it is not evidence of failure but a signal that support needs to be strengthened. By treating these patterns as feedback rather than frustration, leaders keep the change alive rather than letting it decay under pressure.

Finally, celebrate consistency, not perfection. When people see that small, sustained behaviors are acknowledged, they commit more fully. Persistence grows when progress feels visible, valued, and shared.

Persistence proves that transformation has transcended projects and become identity.

Framework Summary: The Four Measures of Visible Change

Measure	Focus	Question	Key Indicators
Perception	Emotional response to change	How do people feel and interpret the change?	Sentiment, trust, confidence, clarity
Participation	Behavioral engagement	Who's showing up and how?	Involvement, dialogue, collaboration, initiative
Performance	Tangible results and outcomes	What's actually improving?	Productivity, quality, well-being, equity

Measure	Focus	Question	Key Indicators
Persistence	Sustainability over time	What endures after attention fades?	Habit formation, retention, continued innovation

When leaders used all four measures, they did not just count outcomes; they *captured meaning*. Measurement became a mirror for growth rather than a grade.

Reflection Prompts

1. What do our current metrics say about what we value most and least?

2. How often do we measure emotion, trust, or belonging alongside performance?

3. What evidence shows that our culture is sustaining change, not only surviving it?

4. When was the last time we measured how people *felt* during change, not only what they *did?*

5. Which area needs more attention in my leadership practice: perception, participation, performance, or persistence?

Measurement is the mirror of leadership. It reflects what we choose to see and what we choose to ignore. When leaders measure only efficiency, they reduce people to numbers. When they measure experience, they elevate numbers into narrative. The future of change leadership is not about collecting more data; it is about collecting *truer stories*.

When perception, participation, performance, and persistence are all tracked together, we see the full face of change, not only the results but also the relationships, emotions, and legacies behind them. Transformation that can be *seen* is easy to celebrate. Transformation that can be *felt* is what endures.

The measure of great leadership is not simply progress on paper. It is people who still believe in the story long after the spotlight fades.

12

THE LEADER'S LEGACY

"But seek first the Kingdom of God and His righteousness, and all these things will be added to you." Matthew 6:33

Legacy: The True Measure of Leadership

Legacy is one of those words that can feel distant, as if it belongs to people who are long gone, carved into marble or remembered in dusty books. But legacy is not a far-off event that begins when your heart stops beating. It is what you are building today, in every word you speak, every choice you make, and every life you touch.

Many leaders assume their legacy will be defined by their achievements: promotions, titles, money in the bank, or awards on the shelf. But here is the truth: buildings crumble, money runs out, trophies rust, and titles fade into history. What never fades is the imprint you leave on people.

I have sat at funerals where speakers listed decades of promotions, committee appointments, and career milestones. Heads nodded politely, but no tears fell. And I have stood at gravesides where the deceased had no wealth or prestige, yet the crowd overflowed into the parking lot. One person after another shared how that individual encouraged them, gave them hope, prayed for them, or showed kindness when no one else would.

That is the difference between a résumé legacy and a relational legacy. One fades quickly; the other echoes for generations.

Lesson: Legacy is not what you leave for people. It is what you leave in people.

Reflection Questions:

> ⇒ If your leadership ended today, would people say you invested more in projects or in people?

> ⇒ Do the things you chase today align with the story you want to tell tomorrow?

> ⇒ What words, actions, or habits of yours will live on in those you lead?

Exercise: The Legacy Mirror
Draw two columns. On the left, list your résumé items: positions,

projects, and possessions. On the right, list the names of people you have influenced.

Step back and look. Which column will matter more when you are gone? Which one are you feeding today?

Organizational Application

Companies should measure not only profit and performance but also people's development. Track mentorship, community impact, and employee growth as carefully as revenue.

The Power of Being Overlooked

Some of the greatest leadership lessons are learned in obscurity. I remember my first men's study group: a room filled with men carrying PhDs in theology and psychology, seasoned preachers who could quote Scripture backward and forward, and elders who had spent decades guiding others. And then there was me, the youngest, the least credentialed, and the least likely to lead.

At first, I questioned everything. Why me? Why would God or anyone place me in this seat? Then I realized that leadership is not about knowing the most; it is about being willing to step forward when others will not.

Being overlooked is not punishment. It is preparation. It teaches humility. It forces you to lead without applause, to serve without the spotlight, and to guide without the guarantee of recognition. Those unseen moments are where leaders are forged.

Lesson: Being overlooked is not a limitation. It is a launchpad.

Reflection Questions:

⇒ Have you ever been overlooked and found strength in it?

⇒ Do you wait for titles to lead, or do you influence where you are?

⇒ Who is quietly overlooked in your circle right now, and how can you call out their potential?

Exercise: Shadow Leadership

Identify one area in your life or organization where you do not hold an official title. This week, influence it anyway. Solve a problem, encourage someone, and serve consistently.

Organizational Application

Rotate facilitation of meetings. Give quieter team members the chance to guide discussions. Overlooked voices often bring the clearest vision.

The Story of Mr. Lightning

This story is hard to tell, but it carries a lesson I will never forget.

Mr. Lightning was a gay man. For that, he was mocked, teased, and bullied. People whispered behind his back, sometimes right in front of him. He carried the silent weight of rejection every day. I still remember the way he walked into a room, shoulders slightly hunched, eyes scanning quickly, as if he could hear every unspoken word people thought about him. Loneliness clung to him like a shadow.

One night, overwhelmed by the weight of isolation, Mr. Lightning ended his life. That night was the last time we saw him. His death left a permanent scar on me, but also a lasting lesson: never walk past people without noticing. Sometimes the cries are silent. Sometimes the pain hides behind laughter, a smile, or a deflection. But it is there.

Leadership is not just about giving direction. It is about listening, not only to words, but to silence, to body language, and to the rhythm of someone's presence.

Lesson: Leadership means hearing what others cannot say out loud.

Reflection Questions:

⇒ Who in your circle might be silently carrying pain right now?

⇒ How can you practice deeper awareness to notice unspoken struggles?

⇒ Are you more focused on completing tasks or caring for the people doing them?

Exercise: Pulse Check

At the start of meetings, ask each person to rate their current state on a scale of 1 to 10. No explanation is needed. Use those numbers as conversation starters. A low number is an invitation to check in privately.

Organizational Application

Build well-being checks into your culture. When people know they are seen, they perform with greater resilience and loyalty.

The Chief and the Sailor Who Rose

In the Navy, the Chief is everything. The Chief is the bridge between what sailors knew before they joined and what they will face in service. The Chief is not just a supervisor. They are a guardian, a counselor, a guide, a mentor, and sometimes the stern hand that shapes a future.

But my first Chief was an unfair coward. He hid behind his position and used authority as a shield instead of a tool. At first, his leadership frustrated me. Eventually, it fueled me. His failure became my motivation to lead with courage where he led with fear.

Years later, I became the first Chief for many sailors. One of them stood out. He was young, motivated, and determined, but one reckless night almost cost him everything. In a place where the drinking age was eighteen, he decided to drink with a group of Marines who had other motives. He drank them under the table but ended up in the hospital.

When I found out, I knew I had a choice. I could let his mistake define him, or I could push him to rise above it. I chose the second path. I mentored him, challenged him, corrected him when needed, and reminded him of his worth and potential.

That sailor did not just recover. He thrived. He rose through the ranks, married, built a family, and today he is Command Master Chief Jordan Jones. Years later, he called to tell me he was applying for the highest enlisted leadership role in the Navy.

His story reminds me of this truth: everything we do matters. Every word of correction, every ounce of belief, and every moment of encouragement echo beyond our sight. They shape lives.

Lesson: The influence you have today may shape someone who outgrows you tomorrow. That is leadership at its finest.

Reflection Questions:

⇒ Who was your first Chief or supervisor, and what did they teach you, good or bad?

⇒ Who are you mentoring right now? Who could one day surpass you?

⇒ How intentional are you about shaping the next generation?

Exercise: Mentorship Map

Write down three people who mentored you. Then list three people you are mentoring now.

Draw arrows between them. That map is your leadership legacy.

Organizational Application

Formalize mentorship programs. Pair veterans with newcomers. Legacy multiplies when everyone becomes both a teacher and a student.

The Church: The Building and the People

Ask young adults why they leave the church, and you will often hear the same answer: a failure of leadership. The church is not a building. It is the people inside. Leadership is not about preserving traditions or structures. It is about creating a place where people can grow, contribute, and lead.

I once led a men's study group where I was the youngest in the room. The others had seminary degrees, doctorates, and decades of preaching experience. I could have been intimidated. Instead, I chose to see them as people, people who, despite all their credentials, still needed encouragement, challenge, and opportunities to lead.

Lesson: Leadership is about creating opportunities for others to lead.

Reflection Questions:

⇒ Do you focus more on protecting structures or empowering people?

⇒ Are you willing to step back to let others step up?

⇒ How can you make your community a place where leadership grows at every level?

Exercise: Opportunity Audit

List five leadership roles in your organization.

Ask yourself, "Who else could lead this role if I stepped aside?"

Then begin intentionally delegating responsibility.

Organizational Application

Develop leadership pipelines. Do not just manage positions. Multiply leaders.

The Power of Seeking

What you seek determines where you lead others.

Matthew 6:33 gives the blueprint:

Seek God's Kingdom and anchor yourself in values that last.

Seek His Righteousness and choose integrity even when shortcuts look tempting.

Seek First and put people above projects and purpose above profit.

Many leaders seek status or recognition, and that is exactly what they get: a shallow following that disappears when the applause stops. But leaders who seek truth, righteousness, and people leave an impact that outlasts them.

Lesson: Direction is determined by desire. What you seek sets the course for everyone you lead.

Reflection Questions:

> ⇒ What am I truly seeking: approval or purpose?

> ⇒ Do my pursuits align with eternal values or temporary applause?

> ⇒ How would my leadership change if I sought the Kingdom first?

Exercise: Value Anchoring

Write down your top three values. For one week, track your decisions against them. Did each decision align with your values or drift from them?

Organizational Application

Define three non-negotiable team values. Evaluate every strategy through that lens.

Put Some "No's" in Your Pocket

Leadership often pressures us into endless yeses. But here is a truth every leader must learn: the most powerful tool in your leadership pocket is the word no.

No keeps your mission focused.

No protects your people from burnout.

No guards your integrity when shortcuts tempt you.

I call it the N.O. Principle:

Navigate Opposition

Negotiate Odds

Nurture Opponents

Notice Outcomes

Nod to Obligation

Noteworthy Optimism

New Onwardness

Lesson: Leaders who know when to say no safeguard what matters most.

The Courage to Hear No

As leaders, we often find ourselves surrounded by people who tell us what we want to hear, not what we need to hear. It feels good to be affirmed. It feels even better to be admired. But affirmation without honesty is dangerous.

Leadership without truth is like navigating through fog with a broken compass. It may feel like movement, but it often leads in the wrong direction.

The best leaders cultivate a circle that values truth over comfort. They understand that leadership is not about being right all the time. It is about making the right decisions, even when those decisions come from hard truths. For that, you need people around you who are brave enough to say no when everyone else says yes. You need people who care more about your growth than your approval.

Hearing no is not rejection. It is protection. It protects your credibility, your integrity, and the people who trust your leadership. The most destructive decisions in history were made in rooms where no one dared to speak up. The opposite is also true. Some of the greatest successes began with a single courageous voice that dared to disagree.

Leaders who surround themselves with truth tellers build organizations grounded in accountability and respect. They invite challenges, welcome correction, and create environments where honesty thrives. They understand that a well-timed no can save a mission, preserve a reputation, and protect a team from unnecessary harm.

True leadership requires the courage to hear what you do not want to hear and the humility to change course when needed. A strong leader does not fear disagreement. They welcome it as a sign of engagement and trust. In the end, the goal is not to always be right. The goal is to get it right.

Reflection Questions:

> ⇒ What is something I have said yes to that should have been a no?

> ⇒ Do I say yes to please people or to pursue progress?

> ⇒ What "no" do I need to say this week to protect what is most important?

Exercise: Stop/Start/Continue:

As a team, identify:

> ⇒ Three things to stop

> ⇒ Three things to start

> ⇒ Three things to continue

Watch how focus sharpens when clarity reigns.

Organizational Application

Companies should practice "strategic no's." Free resources from distractions so you can invest in what aligns with your mission.

Leadership is often mistaken for talking. But I have learned this: listening is leadership in motion. When people feel heard, they feel valued. And when they feel valued, they will follow you further than commands could ever push them.

Lesson: Listening creates trust. Trust builds teams. Teams create transformation.

Reflection Questions:

> ⇒ Do I listen to understand, or just to respond?

> ⇒ Who in my life feels invisible because I have not listened enough?

> ⇒ How do I show others that their words truly matter?

Exercise: Listening Circles

Give each member two uninterrupted minutes to speak.

Others may only reflect what they heard, not respond or correct.

Organizational Application

Create "feedback loops" where team voices actively shape decisions. Listening should not end at hearing; it must lead to action.

Failure as a Teacher

Failure humbles us, but it also refines us. Some of the greatest lessons I have ever learned came through mistakes, setbacks, and struggles.

In the Navy, missions sometimes failed. In business, contracts fell through. In leadership, I made the wrong call. But each failure forced me to ask: *What can I learn here that success could never teach me?*

Lesson: Failure is not final; it is formative.

Reflection Questions:

⇒ What failure has taught me the most enduring lesson?

⇒ Do I see failure as shameful or as a teacher?

⇒ How do I respond when those I lead fail?

Exercise: Failure Review
After each major project, review not only the successes but also the failures. Capture the lesson so you do not repeat it.

Organizational Application
Normalize failure. In innovative teams, a failed experiment is not wasted, it is wisdom gained.

Legacy Through Generations

Your leadership is not measured only by what you accomplish but by who you raise to carry the torch after you.

The story of Command Master Chief Jordan Jones is proof. My mentorship influenced him, but now he influences hundreds of others. And they will influence more still. That ripple effect is legacy.

Lesson: Legacy is generational. You are not just leading followers; you are shaping future leaders.

Reflection Questions:

> ⇒ Who am I mentoring that could one day lead another?

> ⇒ What leader's influence still echoes in my own life?

> ⇒ Am I investing more in immediate results or in future leaders?

Exercise: Generational Leadership Map

Write down two or three leaders who shaped you.

Write down two or three team members you are shaping now.

Draw arrows between them. See the ripple.

Organizational Application

Build succession plans. Leadership is not complete until it outlives you.

The Power of Presence

Sometimes leadership is not about grand speeches or bold strategies. Sometimes it is simply about showing up.

In the Navy, corporate America and in business, I learned that my presence during a crisis calmed my team more than any words could. In church, sitting beside someone in grief meant more than quoting scripture. In corporate America and business, walking the floor during stressful deadlines reassured people more than any email ever could.

Lesson: Presence is more powerful than position.

Reflection Questions:

⇒ Where do I need to show up right now?

⇒ Who needs my presence more than my advice?

⇒ Do I underestimate the power of simply being there?

Exercise: Presence Challenge

Choose one person this week to show up for and support without an agenda. Do not come to fix the situation. Come to be present.

Organizational Application

Leaders should practice "visible leadership", not hiding in offices but walking with their teams during hard times.

4 to 1: Leadership in the Merge

Picture this: you are driving down a four-lane interstate. The speed limit is seventy, but everyone is doing at least eighty. Up ahead, you see the signs: *Left lanes closed. Merge to one.*

Now comes the test. Do you press the gas and squeeze in before the jam, or do you merge early and let others in front of you?

Most people push it, cutting in at the last second and causing more chaos. Few choose the slower, more disciplined path of merging early, allowing room for others, and keeping the flow smooth for everyone. Leadership is no different.

In life, everything comes fast: deadlines, demands, and competing priorities. The lanes start collapsing, and suddenly everything narrows. You cannot avoid the merger, you must decide how to navigate it.

Will you push recklessly to the front, creating chaos for everyone else?

Or will you slow down, merge with wisdom, and make room for others?

Lesson: Leadership is about guiding people through the merge when the lanes are narrowing and the pressure is rising.

Reflection Questions:

⇒ Where in my life are the "lanes merging" right now?

⇒ Am I navigating with courtesy and foresight or pushing for my own gain?

⇒ What does it look like to create smoother paths for those coming behind me?

Exercise: Merge Mapping

Identify three areas in your team or organization where "lanes are merging" such as tight deadlines, overlapping roles, or shifting priorities.

Decide together how to merge responsibilities early to avoid last-minute collisions.

Organizational Application

In high-pressure projects, set clear merge points for responsibilities. Encourage cooperation instead of last-minute scrambling.

Mess vs. Age

Every stage of life comes with its own mess.

When you are young, the mess is inexperience.

In the middle years, it is pressure from raising families, building careers, and managing expectations.

In later years, it is regret or the fear that your time did not matter.

But here is the truth: your mess does not disqualify you. It develops you.

I have seen people at every age bury themselves in shame, believing their mess made them unfit to lead. Yet a mess is often where the message is born. The test of every stage is whether you let your mess silence you or refine your voice.

Lesson: Your mess can become your message.

Reflection Questions:

⇒ What mess in my current stage of life am I afraid to share?

⇒ How could my mess help others if I turned it into a message?

⇒ Do I see my failures as disqualifications or as fuel for leadership?

Exercise: Mess to Message

Write down one personal mess you have faced.

Next to it, write the lesson it taught you.

Then, note one way you could use that lesson to help someone else today.

Organizational Application

Encourage team members to share past "mess to message" lessons from failed projects. Build a culture where setbacks shape future strategy.

Family Leadership: Legacy Begins at Home

It is easy to lead in public and fail in private. The truest measure of leadership begins at home.

I have seen leaders who could move crowds but lost their children. Executives who built companies but neglected their spouses. Pastors who preached powerful sermons but left their families starved of love.

If your leadership fails at home, your legacy loses its anchor.

Leadership in a family is not about perfection. It is about presence. It is about consistency. It is about love.

Lesson: Legacy begins with the people who share your name.

Reflection Questions:

⇒ Am I giving my family the best of me or the leftovers of me?

⇒ What would my spouse or children say about my leadership at home?

⇒ What rhythms can I create that strengthen my family's foundation?

Exercise: Family Audit

Write down your family's needs in three areas: emotional, spiritual, and physical.

Choose one intentional way to meet those needs this week.

Organizational Application

Encourage leaders to share healthy family practices with their teams. Strong families create stronger organizations.

Business Partnerships: Legacy Through Collaboration

Leadership legacy multiplies when it shifts from "me" to "we." Collaboration builds stronger futures than competition ever could.

In my work at E&M Solutions, I have seen how partnerships open doors we could never open alone. When we join forces with others, whether government agencies, churches, or community organizations, our impact multiplies.

Lesson: Legacy grows through collaboration, not isolation.

Reflection Questions:

⇒ Do I see others as competitors or collaborators?

⇒ Who could I partner with to multiply my impact?

⇒ How do I respond when others succeed: with jealousy or celebration?

Exercise: Collaboration List

Write down three potential partners, individuals or organizations.
Identify one way collaboration could expand your reach.
Take the first step to connect.

Organizational Application

Create a collaboration strategy. Identify allies, share resources, and celebrate joint wins.

Community Building: Legacy Beyond the Walls

Legacy is not confined to the home or the office. It spills into the streets, schools, and neighborhoods.

The tiny home initiative I have supported, the youth programs I have helped develop, leading monthly food drives at my church and the community meetings I have attended all remind me that leadership is not about careers. It is about communities.

Lesson: Leadership leaves a mark when it builds communities, not just careers.

Reflection Questions:

⇒ How is my leadership impacting my community beyond my immediate circle?

⇒ What needs exist right outside my door?

⇒ Am I building a legacy that others in my community can feel?

Exercise: Community Connection

Choose one local need your team can serve together, such as school supplies, mentoring, or food drives.

Serve together outside the workplace, then reflect on how it changes you inside.

Organizational Application

Adopt a community project as a team. Serving together strengthens trust and unity.

Leadership and Forgiveness

If you lead long enough, you will be hurt. People will betray you. Projects will fail. You will disappoint others, and they will disappoint you. But forgiveness is the bridge that keeps legacy alive.

Unforgiveness poisons teams. Resentment breeds bitterness. Leaders who carry grudges cannot lead with clarity.

Forgiving others frees you from resentment.
Forgiving yourself frees you from shame.

Forgiveness is not weakness. It is leadership in its purest form.

Lesson: Forgiveness cements legacy with grace, not bitterness.

Reflection Questions:

⇒ Who do I need to forgive to move forward?

⇒ What unresolved moment is still shaping how I lead?

⇒ Do I extend grace as quickly as I expect to receive it?

Exercise: Fresh Start Session

Have each team member share one appreciation and one reset.
Wipe the slate clean and begin again.

Organizational Application

Create a culture where forgiveness is practiced openly. Teams that reconcile grow stronger and trust deeper.

The Life in the Legacy After Death

Death ends a life, but it does not end a legacy.

We all have lost people who shaped us. Our parents, grandparents, children, siblings, mentors, and friends. Their lessons live on through us.

I think of Charlie, my stepfather. A Vietnam veteran, he was a soldier, a worker, and a man who loved photography, motorcycles, and technology. He never met a stranger. His legacy was simple: *do whatever it takes to help those in your path.*

I think of my grandparents Willie B, Ida, Bertha, and Alice, my uncles, aunts, Nephew Austin and cousins who have died. They did not have much by the world's standards, but they had everything that mattered.

Willie B taught me hard work and resourcefulness. Great grandma Ida taught me to be nice to people. Grandma Bertha taught me generosity. Grandma Alice taught me prayer. My aunts and uncles taught to always be their family and those you love. Their legacies live in me every day. And as I grow, I realize their lessons were never meant to stay in the past. They were instructions for how to move through the world, how to show up, how to stand firm, how to love without conditions.

Every decision I make carries a piece of them. Every challenge I overcome echoes their voices. Every time I choose compassion over convenience, strength over fear, or faith over doubt, I honor the people who shaped me long before I had words for who I wanted to be.

Legacy is not just what they left behind it is what continues forward through me. Their values anchor my leadership, influence my relationships, and guide the way I build spaces for others to grow. In many ways, I am their living continuation, the evidence that their lives mattered, and the reminder that ordinary people can leave extraordinary imprints. I am who I am because of them, and the best parts of me are the parts they planted

I think of my great Nephew Mario, a young man who loved cars. He died too soon, but his fascination with how small pieces worked together taught me this: deposit something now so others will have something later.

Lesson: Death is not the end of legacy. Life continues in the stories we live from those who came before us.

Reflection Questions:

> ⇒ Who in my life has left a legacy I still carry?

> ⇒ What specific lessons from them am I living today?

> ⇒ What will live on in others when I am gone?

Exercise: Legacy Stories

Write the name of one person you have lost.
Write the lesson they taught you.
Share that story with someone else this week.

Organizational Application:
Honor past leaders. Share their lessons in team meetings so their influence continues.

Do Not Put Them to Sleep When You Speak

If leadership is a legacy, communication is the vehicle that carries it forward.

Every time you speak, whether in a staff meeting, a sermon, a campaign speech, or a conversation with a child, you are shaping how people remember you. Your words either awaken hearts or lull them into forgetfulness. So do not put them to sleep when you speak.

Every word you share is an opportunity to deliver three things.

1. Something to Think About

When someone dies, we often hear a eulogy. It is not just a speech; it is an invitation to reflect. A eulogy offers comfort, perspective, and sometimes redirection. In those moments of loss, people think more deeply about life, purpose, and impact.

That same energy should live in your words when you speak to others. Speak as if your voice might move someone from darkness to light. Speak with intentionality, as if your words might be the reason someone keeps going. Do not speak to impress. Speak to inspire.

Legacy-building communication begins in the mind. Give them something to think about.

2. Something to Remember

In moments of mourning, we do not just grieve the loss; we remember the moments. A joke. A conversation. A quiet hug. Those small things become the big things in hindsight.

When you speak, tell a story worth repeating. Share something that stays with the heart, not just the head. Your audience may not remember every statistic, slide, or slogan, but they will remember how you made them feel. They will remember the story that made them laugh, the truth that brought tears, or the image that lingered.

Leave them with a story, a truth, or an image they can carry forward. Give them something to remember.

3. Something to Never Forget

Here is the sobering truth: every person you meet will die. So will you. That reality does not make life sad; it makes it sacred.

Do not waste words. Let your message carry weight. Speak from your passion, not just your preparation. Let truth cut through the noise. When you speak, leave behind an echo, a moment they will never forget. When they stand at a crossroads, your words should be one of the voices they hear.

Speak in a way that marks the soul. Give them something to never forget.

Closing Charge: Speak Like a Leader Who Leaves a Legacy

So, when you gather your team,
when you tuck your child in at night,
when you walk into the boardroom, pulpit, courtroom, or community meeting,
do not just speak. Lead.

Let your words be deliberate. Let your stories teach. Let your silence be strategic. Let your tone heal. And let your passion remind people that their lives matter and so does your message.

Every speaking moment has a purpose. Every listener, from your family to your followers, is waiting for a spark. So light it.

Give them three things:

1. Something to think about.

2. Something to remember.

3. Something to never forget.

Then go and give them exactly that.

Infectious Exchange of Energy

There is an exchange of energy in life that cannot be ignored. The way you treat others creates a ripple effect. The energy you release will either heal or harm. It will either lift or break. It will either draw people toward you or push them away.

So, let me say it plainly: just be nice to people.

No matter what they look like.
No matter what they are wearing.
No matter what they represent.
No matter what you think about them.
No matter what you have heard about them.
No matter what you see them do.
And yes, even if they do it to you.

Just be nice to people. Period.

You may ask, "Why?"

Let me tell you why.

About twenty-five years ago, I met a man from a small town in Alabama. He was raised in a home where hate was not hidden; it was taught. Around that family's dinner table, racism was served like the main course. His parents drilled into him: do not trust them, do not like them, do not respect them. Hate them simply because of the color of their skin.

But here is the paradox. This same man grew up with a father who had a friend, an African American man. And every time this boy saw his father's friend, he noticed something remarkable: the man was kind. Always kind. Respectful to everyone. Even to people who rolled their eyes at him. Even to people who mocked him. Even to people who despised him.

Finally, the boy asked, "Why are you always nice to people, even the ones who mistreat you?"

The man's answer was simple but profound:

"Your behavior does not provoke my response."

Think about that. Your behavior does not provoke my response.

That is power. That is self-control. That is leadership.

It takes so much energy to hate. It takes effort to tear someone down. But it takes wisdom and strength to look hate in the face and say: You will not control me. You will not dictate my kindness.

When Hate Shows Up in the Workplace

Fast forward. That boy grew into a man, and years later, I met him. Somewhere along the way, he had forgotten the lesson he once witnessed.

One day, word reached me that he had mistreated one of his employees, a young man from the Philippines. The worker's English was not perfect, but his work was flawless. He was skilled, disciplined, and one of the best at what he did.

Yet he never got a fair chance. Why? Because of the color of his skin.

I called the man into my office. Leadership requires accountability, and accountability often begins with one hard conversation.

I asked him directly, "Did you tell this worker he did not deserve to be here because of his skin color?"

He did not hesitate. He looked me straight in the eye and said, "Absolutely. I told him that. People like him come here, take our jobs, and take our opportunities. And it bothers me."

He said it as if it were obvious, as if prejudice were justified by frustration.

So, I listened. And then I spoke.

"Listen to me," I said. "There is enough work, enough space, and enough opportunity in this country for everyone. Is this not supposed to be the land of the free?"

He fired back, "It is not free when others take what should be mine."

That is when I leaned in. "I have never treated you differently, even though I knew where you came from. You grew up in a racist home, in a racist community. I knew that, yet I never judged you. I never disrespected you. I only asked you to do your job and to treat people with dignity and respect."

He sat in silence. Finally, he said, "Well, that is true. But you are different. You are in charge."

And I told him, "No. We are all in charge. In charge of ourselves. Part of being in charge is choosing to treat people the way we want to be treated. If you think being mistreated is acceptable, then you need to seek counsel. Because it is not acceptable."

The Moral: Leadership Is Measured in Kindness

The moral of the story is simple. Be kind to people. Every chance you get.

Your energy is contagious. Your behavior is infectious. Whether you realize it or not, you are shaping the world around you one interaction at a time.

True leadership is not about numbers, strategy, or vision. It is about the atmosphere you create in every room you enter. It is about the tone you set in every conversation. It is about building a legacy where kindness is not weakness but strength.

Reflection Point

Think about your last week. How many interactions did you have where you could have chosen kindness, even when you did not feel like it?

How many times did you allow someone else's negativity to provoke your response?

Leadership legacy is not just about what you achieve in the boardroom. It is about how you shape the atmosphere in the room.

Let your energy be infectious in the best possible way. Leave people better than you found them. That is how leaders build legacies that last.

Blending Legacy into Purpose: E&M Solutions

When we started E&M Solutions, it was never about contracts or numbers. It was about impact.

Through accurate research, careful data, and intentional strategy, we set out to transform the landscape of homes, communities, and even our country.

We have every skill, credential, and tool to succeed, but success is not defined by money. Success is people transformed. Success is communities strengthened. Success is leaders being built at every level.

Lesson: When chaos or confusion closes in, do not wait for clarity. Lead your way out.

Reflection Questions:

> ⇒ How does our mission align with the legacy we want to leave?

> ⇒ Are we measuring success by contracts or by people?

> ⇒ What impact will our work have on homes and communities twenty years from now?

Exercise: Mission Alignment

At your next team meeting, ask: "Did today's decisions align with our mission?"
Keep that accountability front and center.

⇒ **Three Final Reflection Questions:**

⇒ When people speak of my leadership years from now, what will they say I invested in most, projects or people?

⇒ Who am I mentoring right now who could carry forward a part of my legacy?

⇒ If my leadership ended today, what story would others talk about me?

Closing Charge

A leader who knows when to say yes is efficient.
A leader who knows when to say no is effective.
A leader who knows when to seek first leaves a legacy.

Remember Marcus. Remember the Chief. Remember Command Master Chief Jordan Jones. Remember the church that is not a building but the people within it. Remember Charlie, Willie B, Great grandma Ida, Grandma Bertha, Grandma Alice, Austin and Mario. Remember the power of being overlooked and rising anyway. Remember that listening, failure, generations, presence, merging, family, partnerships, community, forgiveness, death, and even your mess all shape the message you leave behind.

And remember this: Seek first the Kingdom of God and His righteousness, and everything else will fall into place. Everything we do matters. And everything that matters, we must do. That is legacy.

Remember that listening, failure, generations, presence, merging, family, partnerships, community, forgiveness, death, and even your mess all shape the message you leave behind.

And remember this: Seek first the Kingdom of God and His righteousness, and everything else will fall into place. Everything we do matters. And what matters most, we must do. That is legacy.

DEDICATION

This book is dedicated to the brave men and women who have worn the uniform of our nation with honor, courage, and unwavering commitment. You have stood watch in times of peace and borne the weight of battle in times of war. You have protected freedoms many will never fully understand, and you have paid a price that can never truly be repaid.

Your service is not just in the past; it echoes every opportunity we seize, every mission we complete, and every life we touch. The lessons you have learned discipline, sacrifice, resilience, and leadership under pressure are the very principles that inspire these pages. May this work serve as a testament to the truth that leadership is a testament that leadership is not about position, but ensuring every do their part to make a difference.

You are the living embodiment of leading at every level. Whether on the front lines, in the command center, or quietly guiding from the shadows, your leadership has shaped history and safeguarded freedom. You have led without seeking glory, served without expecting recognition, and sacrificed without the world ever entirely knowing your face. This is the essence of authentic leadership standing ready when called, delivering when needed, and carrying the weight of responsibility with quiet strength.

This book is a tribute to that spirit. Your courage, resilience, and unwavering commitment remind us that leadership is not defined by rank or title, but by the choices we make when the world is watching and even more so when it is not. May these pages written by six veterans reflect the timeless truth you have lived: when nothing has a face, leadership becomes the face that guides the way. With enduring gratitude and respect, we honor you.

www.ingramcontent.com/pod-product-compliance
Lightning Source LLC
Chambersburg PA
CBHW030405130626
46549CB00004B/1642